DEAR, DEAR
BRENDA

DEAR, DEAR BRENDA

The Love Letters of
Henry Miller to
Brenda Venus

•

Text by Brenda Venus
Edited by Gerald Seth Sindell

A CORWIN/SINDELL PRODUCTION

•

WILLIAM MORROW AND COMPANY, INC.
New York

Copyright © 1986 by Brenda Venus and Corwin/Sindell Productions

All rights reserved. No part of this book may be reproduced or utilized in any form
or by any means, electronic or mechanical, including photocopying, recording or by any
information storage and retrieval system, without permission in writing from the Publisher.
Inquiries should be addressed to Permissions Department, William Morrow and Company, Inc.,
105 Madison Ave., New York, N.Y. 10016.

Library of Congress Cataloging-in-Publication Data

Miller, Henry, 1891–
Dear, dear Brenda.

1. Miller, Henry, 1891–   —Correspondence.
2. Venus, Brenda—Correspondence. 3. Authors,
American—20th century—Correspondence.
4. Love-letters. I. Venus, Brenda. II. Sindell,
Gerald Seth. III. Title.
PS3525.I5454Z497   1986   818'.5209 [B]   85-15424
ISBN 0-688-02816-0

Printed in the United States of America

First Edition

1 2 3 4 5 6 7 8 9 10

BOOK DESIGN BY BERNARD SCHLEIFER

Dᴀᴠɪᴅ A. Hᴏꜰꜰᴍᴀɴ

*A giant among men, a true friend, and inspiration to
all artists in the dawn of their creativity.
Without his unwavering support, encouragement and
guidance this book would not have been possible*

Special thanks to:

CORWIN/SINDELL

*Stan Corwin—another Scorpio who shared my vision, and
Gerry Sindell—a man of heart and tremendous sensitivity*

*whose combined effort and perception for style, placement,
and flow transformed four thousand pages of letters
to reflect the simple truth of my "affair of the heart,"
and surely one Henry Miller would have been
as proud of as I am. I am grateful that your elegant taste
in subject matter brought you to my front door;
your expertise in the publishing world has opened my eyes
to a new and exciting life—one both of you made possible.*

PAT GOLBITZ

*A lovely lady, enthusiastic and professional.
I was pleased to know that the work I loved so much
would end in her kind and caring hands.*

PREFACE

IT WAS AFTER A separation of some ten years that a happy accident enabled me to catch up with Henry Miller, my old friend. This stroke of good fortune was the offer of the Andrew Mellon lectures at the prestigious California Institute of Technology in Pasadena. I realized that if I accepted I should be living within a few kilometres of Miller and more or less the same distance from Anaïs Nin. It was a marvelous opportunity to reforge and revive an old and important friendship which was showing signs of fatigue and neglect, subject as it was to the hazards of distance and time. Thus I strayed into the camera's field (so to speak) roughly at the halfway point in the present correspondence.

Miller himself had lots to tell me about Brenda Venus, and never a day passed without him scribbling a message to her. The thought of her was omnipresent. He does not exaggerate when he says she is literally keeping him alive; indeed, her generosity and tact allowed him to end his days in a marvelous euphoria of loving attachment. This correspondence is the fruit of that deep "affair of the heart"—the phrase comes aptly enough because given his age and the precarious state of his health it could hardly have been anything else. He was, as he himself writes, a physical ruin. Then when the young actress strayed into his life a wind stirred the embers of Mona, of June, Betty, Anaïs—and he once more became the young lover and renegade of his early books. What luck! Everyone was absolutely delighted for him, not the least his children and friends, because any foreseeable alternative that might present itself was dire in the extreme. He would have been forced to drowse away his last years with the needle and knockout drops for company! Poor Henry! As it was, he lived them in an ecstasy of love bequeathed, valued, and reciprocated. Brenda Venus played the finest role an actress could wish for—Muse and Nurse of a great spirit in his decline. What luck that she arrived when she did. And what luck that she was a girl of sensibility and compassion and fully capable of living up to the importance of her role.

Miller had just emerged from an unlucky misadventure in marriage with the delightful Japanese pianist Hoki, and his self-confidence was as badly shaken as his health. He has given a moving and vivid account of this period in *Insomnia: or the Devil at Large*, so there is no need to repeat the details.

With the arrival of Brenda Venus everything changed. There was not a moment of the day when he did not think of her, worry about her, refer to her—indeed his conversation was starred with references to her qualities of heart and mind. And almost as frequently he broke off whatever he might be doing to write her a line. He was very conscious that his life was on the ebb. He had maintained an obstinate silence about his operations—one of them lasted sixteen hours. But his vivacity of mind and heart rendered him so buoyant and gay that one was deceived into thinking him much younger than he was. It was only when I saw him in the flesh that I realized how fragile and thin he had become. An artificial artery like a piece of garden hose, linking his heart system to a vein in his thigh throbbed ominously in his neck and breast. For a great walker—he used to be unhappy if he walked less than ten kilometres a day, and in Paris he always walked everywhere; for such a man, he was now totally bedridden! And to cap it all he was completely blind in one eye and all but so in the other. Bearing these infirmities in mind, the reader should now turn to the correspondence—he will think he is reading the exuberant work of a man of forty. Such humor and such ardor speak volumes for the tender friendship and devotion of his last love.

Inevitably a correspondence of such a nature and at such close range for the most part will have a few shortcomings such as repetitiousness or even blanks when the authors were meeting daily; there are also passages which might cause some squeamishness on the reader's part, for there is much that is outspoken here; Miller sometimes reverts to what he once called his "anatomical" style, as in *Sexus*; but Miss Venus rode out these storms with quiet patience and persistence—which should clearly show how much she cared for her friendship with him, and how precious he was for her as a mentor. Indeed anyone who knew him will attest that he was a captivating human being despite his unpredictable maverick moments. And here, as in his autobiographical books, he provides us with a portrait in the round of himself on the threshold of death.

The role of Brenda Venus will keep its interest and importance also as a memorial of his last great attachment—an Ariel to his Prospero, one might say. She enabled him to dominate his infirmities and to experience all the joys of Paradise. How grateful we all are for her kindness and loving insight!

—Lawrence Durrell

March, 1983
Paris

ACKNOWLEDGMENTS

MY FAMILY, MY FOUNDATION for life and love. I pray to God that they will understand. Lawrence Durrell, thank you for your wisdom, poetic sensitivity, true love of Henry Miller, and the great honor of getting to know you and your marvelous humor. Yuri Smalztoff, my brother, if not by blood, by something much stronger. An understanding of survival, a bond of faith, hope, and unselfish love. Henry Bushkin, a gentleman with style, a brilliant mind, benevolent, a true and loyal friend. Thank you for all you have done and for the thorough work of Leanna and Jill. Pamela Phillips Oleand, contributions straight from the heart and discovering the book's title through a dream that became a reality. Georges Hoffman, a tremendous help in the conceptual steps and who introduced me to the warmth of Henry Miller's Paris. Jeff Robin, just by being himself showed me that the business world can also have integrity and trust. Nate Sassover, his astute insight and belief in the greatness of Henry Miller found the perfect package of Corwin-Sindell.

EDITOR'S NOTE

VIRTUALLY EVERY ONE OF the more than fifteen hundred letters Henry Miller wrote Brenda Venus contains some sentence or paragraph that merit inclusion in this book. But a compendium of selected fragments, no matter how interesting each might be on its own, would fail to convey the unique flavor of this remarkable love story. Hoping to preserve the vitality, diversity, and depth Miller brought to his affair with Brenda, we have built the narrative entirely from complete letters. On many occasions Miller wrote Brenda two and three times a *day*, and only in sampling the force of this torrent can we comprehend the extent to which he was truly living for her.

Deletions within the letters have been few, and made primarily to diminish redundancy. A scholarly edition, if there were to be one, would differ in completeness, not substance.

My personal thanks to Allyn Johnston for her meticulous transcription of the originals, to Stan Corwin for his unique ability to discern objects in the fog which become clear to the rest of us only subsequently, to Pat Golbitz for her sensitivity and guidance, to Brenda for her trust in this process and for her courage in sharing with all of us this private and cherished part of her life, and finally to Henry Miller, whom I have encountered through these letters, for his passion.

G.S.S.

1976

•

The night I was going to hear Henry Miller speak at an acting class, my house burned down. I didn't go to the lecture, but a few weeks later I still wanted to meet him. I began to ask around for his address so I could write to him. At the same time, I was trying to refurnish my home. At an estate auction I discovered a first-edition set of books titled *Women Through the Ages*. I took out one of the volumes, and there folded inside was a letter from Henry Miller to a woman. How could I *not* bid on the books? Three thousand dollars later I owned them and had Miller's address. I wrote him, enclosing the letter I had found, as well as a few "actress" photographs of myself that I thought might pique his curiosity.

A few days later, Henry sent the first of the fifteen hundred letters he was to write me. We became good friends and, perhaps, even more.

BRENDA VENUS

•

June 9, 1976

Dear Brenda—

Is it really "Venus"? I couldn't make it out but my secretary says that's what you wrote. A little unbelievable! Are you an actress? Is that your real name or a pseudonym? From your photo you could be an actress—and perhaps with a little Spanish or Mexican blood. In any case, very lovely.

I wonder why you would want to see an 84 year old writer like me?

17

(Incidentally, too bad you missed the session at the Lab. It went off great. Do you know Jack Garfein who runs the Lab?)

Sure I'd be happy to meet you, always glad to see a beautiful woman. I am in bed a good deal because of my legs—arthritis and sclerosis. So I might greet you in pajamas and bathrobe. I'll call you after I hear from you again.

If you are as beautiful as your photo then *Je vous embrasse tendrement.*

HENRY MILLER

•

Before I could write back, Henry wrote again.

•

6/10/76

Dear Brenda Venus!

I found the letter you enclosed—thank you! Yes, it was from Juney Lim, half Japanese, half Chinese. Glad to have it. Do try to think how this letter could possibly have gotten into an old book of yours. There must be *some* connection. Juney was a bit actress now and then—also connected (later) with porno film makers. Very bright, very attractive. Knew a lot of people about town.

You said you were from Mississippi. Did you ever hear of a small town there named Kosciusko? There is a book store there which handles my books—but not the "obscene" ones. I rarely get a letter from the deep South. Guess I'm too "vulgar" for them. Have *you* read my books? More anon.

Cheers!

HENRY MILLER

6/13/76

Dear Brenda—

Got your two missives. Surprised to know you had a photo of me on your door.

That fire which cleaned you out reminds me that the same thing happened to Aldous Huxley. And he had the same reaction. Felt relieved of the burden of possessions!

You sound like a very serious young woman. That you love your mother also surprises me. Most young women hate their mother nowadays.

I hated my mother like poison. Never got over it. But if you have read my work—have you? I guess you know the story.

You don't say whether you drive and have a car or not. I'd love to go to dinner with you soon.

HENRY

6/16/76

Dear Brenda Love—

I tried to take a nap. My day is ruined—in a beautiful way. After reading your two letters and gazing again and again at your lovely photos I can't work, I can only dream. And since I have no wonderful photos to send you I send you other things. I wish I could fold myself up and mail myself in an envelope to you!

I snapped out of a half-hearted sleep thinking—if she can write me two letters at one time I can do the same or better.

You say you like my handwriting. Yes, Brenda, I do all my writing by hand ever since I lost the sight in my good right eye. I lost it during a by-pass operation for my artery—was on the table too long (16 hours!) and the optic nerve became paralyzed. A great handicap as it curtails my reading, writing, and painting. (I did paint half-a-dozen water colors after the loss of the eye, but have lost the inclination to paint. I must have painted several thousand.) Fortunately, one cannot tell I am blind in one eye—it moves with the other one—no disfigurement.

You mention some interesting names. Baudelaire, for example. Did you really read him? And have you ever read Rimbaud? I wrote a book about the latter called *The Time of the Assassins.* (Very timely, what!) My favorites are all Europeans, with the exception of Isaac Bashevis Singer—I hope you've read him?

Did I tell you I shall soon be made a member of the Legion of Honor? In Paris the prostitutes demonstrated against the award, saying I treated them unfavorably, whereas I thought I had done very well by them. And here the Women's League protested at the French Embassy in Washington, D.C.—"I am a dirty chauvinist pig," say they. The truth is just the contrary. I love women and consider them superior to men. It's men who create war and other terrible things—torture, for example.

I get many letters from young French women. They are very intelligent, very perceptive—and more alert than American women, I find. Women, women . . . , there are now six on my string, so to speak— three being Oriental.

You know, Brenda, at first glance I thought you might be rather cold. Today I studied your mouth—it was more inviting than I had thought before. Of course, as you know only too well, your eyes are like great shining orbs—and very soft, very seductive. I keep wondering which of the three bloods in you rule the roost. I hope it's the Sicilian. (They have hot blood. The Indian is rather cold, I think.)

The enclosed blurb about the *Nightmare Notebook* is merely to arouse your curiosity, not to sell you. It was on that yearlong Nightmare trip around America that I had some wonderful experiences in the deep South. Strange that no Southern belle ever tempted me. (Perhaps I found them a little too artificial and self-centered.) I am always inclined to think of the Southern belle as a flirt and a tease, romantic but insincere. Please change my mind! Enuf now. This time I kiss you in some unknown area.

HENRY

•

I was intrigued but not surprised by how swiftly Henry began to write intimately. It was exciting and fun for me to send him various photos from films and modeling jobs. Using a magnifying glass, he would analyze and comment on each one. It brought us close together even before we met.

•

June 16, 1976

Dear Brenda—

What a surprise! You *are* generous—or is it vanity? All those photos and you are more stunning in each one. (I like the little mole on your cheek! Don't you also have one elsewhere on your body? Pure intuition on my part.)

You ask if I ever knew Nietzsche or Sartre? No! Nietzsche was dead, I believe, before I was born. As for Sartre, I like his plays but not his novels or his philosophy. Do you?

About the kite. Funny, in Big Sur I flew kites—only there was a terrible downdraft in the canyons and the kites would get torn or lost. I always admired the old Chinese men (often writers or philosophers) who flew kites in their old age while their sing song girls watched and clapped hands.

Unfortunately, I don't go to the beach anymore. Trudging through the sand is too hard on my legs. I can barely walk a few yards on level ground, with a cane and leaning on someone's arm. I have arthritis in one hip and arteriosclerosis in one leg.

In one of the photos (I take it it was from a film) a man is bent over your hand as if to kiss it and back of him is a man scowling ferociously. Who is or was he? And is that Clint Eastwood you are sitting with at the sea shore? You sent me two just of your head. They are the best. In one of them you have a slight smile. It gets me. I feel you are looking at *me*. But what a melting look! In this one I can *faintly* see the "Collar of Venus." How fetching!

Keep sending me photos if you can. I love them! In the absence of you (in the flesh) I can talk to these and kiss and hug them, without so much as asking your permission. At my age we men are more suscepti-ble than ever to feminine charms. Never get enough.

Enuf now or I'll go on and on. I hope you are over the cold. If only for your lover's sake! (Don't believe it!) Where shall I kiss you, dear Brenda? I like your tiny belly button. I'll plant one there, by your leave.

HENRY

I write the rest in my sleep. There we have no censor! I repeat, you are absolutely bewitching. How does one get that way? You must have had wonderful parental love for you seem to be all love.

June 17, 1976

Dear Brenda—

It's only a little after nine but I can't sleep. You've bewitched me! Now that I know you are a Scorpio I must be very wary or my heart will be broken to bits. I am a sucker for Scorpio women, as you must have surmised already.

To begin with, I feel guilty making advances in your direction. To tell the truth, I am deeply in love with a woman—an actress also, only Chinese!—for the last ten years. It is an "eternal" love—and I mean that seriously. But I am a man, even if 84 years old, and am always in love with some one or two or three or four. Still, this time I feel as if I am betraying my love. But, probably because you are a Scorpio, and extremely beautiful, and from the deep South, I am unable to resist you. I want to advance and retreat at the same time. What can I give a young woman like you? It seems to me I can only take—and at my age that's doubly disgraceful. Still, I am sure we are going to meet in the flesh—and soon. Perhaps you may even allow me to hold you in my arms—briefly. (?) That collar of Venus intrigues me. I can't help it, since I know what it means.

I am awaiting your letter. Your voice over the phone is very light and now and then I miss a word or a phrase.

I am trying to figure out where your neighborhood is. The reason? Because soon I would like to have you for dinner at the Imperial Gardens, the Japanese restaurant just below the Chateau Marmont on Sunset. That is, if you don't mind picking me up and driving me there. I don't drive and have no car. Do you know how to get to my place? Take Sunset Blvd. Go toward the ocean until you come to an intersection at Chautauqua Blvd. Turn left there, go 2 blocks, then right 2 *short* blocks to Ocampo and I am the third house from the corner, lefthand side of street. House has a balcony. Is that clear? And could you do that sometime? I have been going to this restaurant for quite a few years. It's where I met Hoki, my Japanese wife.

Well, I've spilled the beans, as they say. Now it's your turn.

I'm sorry to seem as if I were rushing you, but that's only because you are so tempting, so seductive, so irresistible.

I may be thoroughly disappointing to you. If so, then let's get it over with quickly!

Now, I'm going back to bed. I'll be thinking of you in bed also, and I will conduct an imaginary conversation with you. How's that for pro tem?

Je t'embrasse encore une fois et plus tendrement.

HENRY MILLER

6/21/76

Dear Brenda—

Tried to phone you at your home toward 7:00 P.M. this evening. A man answered the phone curtly and gruffly. Thought maybe I got the wrong number, so I hung up. Sorry.

Showed my daughter Val your photos this evening. She thought you were extraordinarily beautiful. She knew the *Eiger Sanction* film. Wondered what you wanted of me (sic)! Hope to hear from you soon.

HENRY

6/25/76

Dear Brenda—

Are you still around? I've called several times but always miss you, as you do me. Cross currents! My son Tony tells me he saw *The Eiger Sanction* (he's an Eastwood fan!) and said if you played the part of the Indian woman you were great—and that you had a gorgeous body!! Does that please you?

All the best!

HENRY

Sweating to death these days!!

Saturday—6/26/76

My dear Brenda (or the Botticelli of Mississippi)—

Doesn't make sense, does it, but sounds good . . .

Dear Brenda, I got four letters in a row from you today. Marvelous!

You mention my fingers—yes, they once played the piano and they have strummed many a tune on a woman's private parts. You know, getting a flood of mail from a beauty like you tends to make me feel a bit horny, forgive the expression.

In your first letter, you talk of paying me a visit some afternoon and going to dinner in your Porsche. (I wouldn't mind if it were only a V.W.) O.K., dear Brenda—some day or eve this coming week—possibly Thursday or Sunday next: Imperial Gardens where they treat me royally.

I have taken quite a few beautiful women there, but you should take the cake. I love dark hair and skin. What color are your eyes—heliotrope?

P.S. Have to make this short—expect a visitor. May write again this evening. Tried to phone you a little while ago (2:00 P.M.). Took a chance on finding you home today. Hugs and kisses and embraces, etc.

HENRY

Tuesday Night 6/29/76

Dear Brenda—

It wasn't vanity that prompted me to leave a message with your answering service this evening. I thought you may never have seen this short film and it might amuse you.

Tonight I feel my soul expanding, or, to be more truthful, I am aware that I do indeed possess a soul.

Which reminds me that I had a long correspondence and a very intimate one with a most beautiful Japanese young woman (not Hoki!) who was a feminist, an active one, in Japan.

She came to see me finally and while talking about my soul held my penis in her hand. It was sheer bliss.

Somehow or other I am also aware tonight that I am a world figure. I belong to the world, not to America or France. I can think this way without my ego becoming swollen.

Listen, Thursday a French friend of mine, who is the distributor, is giving me a private screening of the most erotic film ever made in Japan. The title is in French—L'Empire de Sens. I wish you were seeing it with me.

Nearly all the very beautiful women I have known seemed to lack confidence in themselves. "Beauty is only skin deep," the saying goes. What these women fear is that they do not have the character to match their beauty. Often they become frigid or almost. I was glad to learn you have always been in love. I know men, even French men, who never touched a woman until they were over 21. When you begin to fuck is not the all important, but how you do it. With heart and soul or just your cunt.

I told you the collar of Venus was significant. So your whole body is one erogenous zone. How marvelous! (By the way it's not "reoccurring," but "recurring." I hope it disappears soon.) Fevers are dangerous. The only permissible fever is the fever of love. Or as some French author—De Maupassant, I believe—said: "The best part of love is walking up the stairs."

To change the tune: Have you seen any of Lina Wertmuller's films? *Swept Away*, perhaps? There's a woman I admire, as I do Germaine Greer. Both more frank, more daring, more courageous than most men. And both extremely capable. Lina, in my opinion, is a better director than any man. When I saw *Swept Away* I was reminded of *Tropic of Cancer* and *Sexus*. Humor and fucking—lots of it . . . a belly full. Hollywood doesn't give us that, for all the stars they have.

To answer about the Orient: No, I have never been to Japan, China, or India, but they are familiar as if from an earlier incarnation. Here is what I said about the Japanese woman in a deluxe edition of *Insomnia* (Japanese version): "It would seem to me that the Japanese woman was put on this earth to introduce a note of beauty and joy in a world which men from the beginning of time have tried to make ugly and unlivable."

Does that tell you anything? I think the French woman is wonderful because she is the equal of her man and participates in all his activities. Have you ever noticed how poor we Americans are at the art of conversation? Not the French! No sir!

Well, my most beautiful, most exquisitely beautiful Brenda, keep sending me photos, always revealing a little more.

I returned your call last night about 10:30 but you did not answer. Were you out or in bed with another lover? (Have you ever answered the phone while having intercourse—or put the receiver between your legs?)

From "the other incurable Romantic," Ta ta—*Bonne Nuit!*

H.M.

Thursday and Friday nights I am invited out to dinners. Did you ever hear of Lorenzo Music? Almost as distinctive as Brenda Venus, what! Enuf now. No more paper. Good night. Let your soul wander in dream.

HENRY

Noon 7/1/76

Dear Brenda,

Can't write much—visitors due for lunch and take others to Imperial Gardens tonight. But I promised to tell you about the Japanese film last night.

Well, I was thoroughly deceived. In my opinion it was a porno but tricked up with story line and strong sexual love between the two. Actually, it's based on a true story which I have known about for years but they elaborated, altered, and exaggerated.

When it was over, I told the man who showed me it that I hated it. The script could have been written by the defunct Marquis de Sade. They try every position, and use the dildo once—very painful. The woman is a pure nymphomaniac who actually goes mad sexually at the end. She strangles him to death slowly while on top of him. This is supposed to be the acme of sexual gratification. And after he's dead she cuts off his penis, wanders around with it in her kimono, and then surrenders to the police. I didn't have a single sexual emotion nor the least flutter of the heart throughout—yet I never saw anything like it before.

I think the Japs have an obsession about sex and death. It occurs over and over again. Witness Mishima.

The sub-titles were in English, not French. It will be showing in movie houses here soon. I doubt that Americans will like it however crazy they are about sex and violence.

In one scene there is an old woman of 70 watching the two fuck. His girl suggests he give the old woman a treat. So he proceeds to give her a real honest-to-God fuck. In the midst of it the old woman dies.

Time and again his lover stops him—anywhere—to say she wants it, she can't wait, do it here now! He says, "But people can see us." She replies, "I don't care." A real maniac of sex. Yet it doesn't rouse you or make you come in your pants.

After the movie taken to the St. Germain—French restaurant on Melrose and Cahuenga. Superb meal! Ever go there?

Must stop now. Mail hasn't come yet. Like you, I'm always waiting for the mail, tho' most of it is boring fan mail!

Here's the mail now! Let's see if there's another from *you*.

HENRY

Saturday—7/3/76

Dear Brenda—

No letter from you but some glorious photos. Thank you so much. The naked one with the child—not *your* child, is it? Were you posing in imitation of some famous painting? I always love the ones just of your head—you are *so* beautiful! Not that I find anything wrong with your body! But your face haunts me.

By the way, in the photo with the child the expression in your eyes is totally different. You look like another person!

I wish you had enclosed a little note. Though your handwriting is abominable, as I told you before, I like to catch the "murmurs of your heart"! (Did you ever see that French film by Louis Malle—*Murmur of the Heart?*)

Last night, as I wrote you in my last letter, I went to Scandia's for a birthday dinner. It was fabulous. (My first time there.) I put it above the best French restaurants in L.A.!! Only, what gluttons shoving down their gullets this marvelous food. I suppose you have been taken there many times? When I mention Imperial Gardens it must seem like small fry to you, but I love not only the Japanese cuisine but the ambience *and* the Japanese waitresses—some of them, more especially the hostess, Chizuko, who is rather tall for a Japanese and has a willowy figure. I hope she'll be there the night we go together.

Well, dear Brenda, I hope no incubus is disturbing your sleep now. Substitute yours truly for the demon, if you can.

When will we meet? After the 4th, I hope. If you could come around 4:30 to 5:00 and take me to Imperial Gardens one day, fine (preferably Thursday or Sunday), fine and dandy.

Oh yes, a little thing, but may amuse you. When I was 16, my father took me (for the first time) to a New York theatre—a regular drama. The piece was—*A Gentleman from Mississippi* and *who* played the part, if I remember rightly, but Fatty Arbuckle, the comedian who was charged with trying to shove a coke or beer bottle up some poor girl's cunt. Isn't that a strange one? I have been going to the theatre since 7 or 8 years of age. I loved the vaudeville at the Palace *and* Minsky's Burlesk on Houston St. June or Mona (my 2nd wife) played with the Theatre Guild in the 1920's.

Enuf of this. I am getting as garrulous as an old woman.

Thank you again so much for the lovely photos. (I don't like you with glasses. Don't wear 'em!)

P.S. You are very generous. Unusual in women! *Don't* give yourself too recklessly. Wait till their tongues hang out! Write me soon, or are you writing me *now*, perchance?

HENRY

July 4, 1976

Dear Brenda—

I have been trying to sleep it off like a bad dream, as I told the *L.A. Times,* but I can't do it. I'm slept out—and yet I believe I <u>can</u> sleep some more, just for lack of anything better to do.

I have three unfinished chapters on my desk and my paints and brushes are all spread out on the ping pong table, but I can't bring myself to tackle anything. I'm like an empty douche bag!

All I think of is *you*, you, you. And your telephone number—273-1518 over and over and over. You see what a potent spell your photos weave! I see the Indian in you very strongly now and then the Sicilian—*in the eyes.* They all speak of love. Your whole being radiates love. You are like Botticelli's "Venus Rising from the Sea." You are all scintillating foam and sea weed. Your look comes from the depths, not from Mississippi. You are not real. You are a dream of a dream. And I am frantically reaching out to snatch it.

I read somewhere recently that every eel in the world is born in the Sargasso Sea. After it gets to be a year or two old it swims through thousands of miles of oceans to live in the rivers where they were conceived. Why do I tell you this? I don't know. My son wants to have a reason for everything he does. I abhor reason and logic. I do things, write things, to find out why I wanted to do them. For me all is the joy of discovery. The world was born yesterday; it will vanish tomorrow. "*Le bel aujourd'hui,*" as my friend Blaise Cendrars used to say.

So today, *qui n'est pas si bel,*—I am giving up to you . . . If I get up enough courage and wits I will call you later today, never expecting to catch you in. I hope you have written me or are writing me. I want to see a letter or two or three from you in the mail box Tuesday. I need you like sin (strange expression, isn't it?).

I have a fan in New Guinea who keeps sending me strange photos like the enclosed in his letters. Can you imagine *wearing* that as a mask?

Your mouth is so inviting!!! Forgive my unspoken desires.

HENRY

•

For almost a month we had been writing at least daily, but still hadn't met face to face!

One afternoon the phone rang and it was Henry calling to arrange a time to pick him up for dinner that night. I chose an emerald-green dress, thinking the color would please him.

I drove to his house, was let in by a housekeeper and Henry's bedroom was pointed out to me. I walked into his bedroom and found him snoozing. I stood in the doorway for a moment or so until he opened his eyes. He said, "Brenda, is that you? For a moment I thought you were an apparition!"

I went closer to him and smiled. Somehow, I felt I had known him all my life.

•

July 5, 1976

My dear Brenda—

You're as real as a cat! I was delighted to find a replica in the flesh of that extraordinary beauty of the photos. I hope you found the evening as wonderful as did I. In German we would say—*Ausgezeichnet* or *Fabelhaft!!!!*

Today, to my surprise, came another letter from you. (Let me say that the letter you wrote in the dark at the theatre was as legible as any of your previous ones.)

I have been answering letters for the last few hours. What a chore! Now I can breathe! I don't have to write you, it's a joy. (Only I'm a bit pooped.) No matter. What impressed me about you was your authenticity, your sincerity and integrity. Another woman, having your experiences, would have had her wings burned, or at least singed. Like Rimbaud—you remain *"intact"* (or I hope so!).

Also, I must tell you, never did I get the thrill in putting my arms around a woman such as your athletic, elastic, firm body gave me. I was thunderstruck. I could have sunk to my knees and felt you all over indiscriminately. (Presumptuous, eh?) In a sense we talked ourselves silly. Yet I feel there is so much more in both of us to reveal to one another. (You are a good listener, incidentally.)

Oh, yes, by the way, those stories I told you about Anaïs Nin, I hope you will never betray me and retell them. It would break my heart. Especially now, dying as she is.

You're so sensible—and a thinker in the real sense. You may have acquired much from books and from your quondam Maecenas, but it comes out like one's very own. Easy, natural, too.

The girl from Mississippi has gone through a great evolution. And, under difficult circumstances! Bravo! I salute you!

And now I close with an imaginary hug and warm kisses.

HENRY

Saturday 7/9/76

Dear Brenda—

It seems strange not to find a letter from you today. You have spoiled me.

You know what gave me a bit of a thrill the other night? Passing near your residence. I wish you had made a detour so that I could have seen it close up.

Brenda, what is the name and address again, please, of your favorite little restaurant? I want to go there sometime and see for myself.

I just received word from a young woman journalist that her friend Francis Coppola *(The Godfather)* will be back in L.A. for a week or so very soon and that he would like to meet me and take me to dinner. Do you know him at all? How are you these days? I miss you. I adore you body and soul.

HENRY

•

Henry's house was a simple, white, spacious two-story dwelling with a perfectly manicured lawn. Since he knew I loved gardenias, he bought several bushels of gardenia plants to frame the entrance of his door. On the front door was pasted:

When a man has reached old age and has fulfilled his mission, he has a right to confront the idea of death in peace. He has no need of other men, he knows them already and has seen enough of them. What he needs is peace. It is not seemly to seek out such a man, plague him with chatter, and make him suffer banalities. One should pass by the door of his house as if no one lived there.

—MENG TSE

The door itself was painted black. To the right near the stairway was a portrait in oil of Henry and one of his daughter, Val. Down the hall to the left on the wall was an exotic black-and-white picture of Ava Gardner, a close friend of his. And near the entrance of the kitchen was a mysterious and haunting portrait of June Smith, his ex-wife that somewhat resembled Greta Garbo. To the right, going toward Henry's bedroom, were several watercolors that he had done in earlier years, and also a photograph of Anaïs Nin.

I loved his bedroom, maybe because we had many great talks and shared many secrets there. It was a comfortable room and the prettiest in the house. It smelled like a newborn baby's room. On the old brass bed was a cream-colored satin quilt. Very elegant. Above the bed was a large painting, which was later replaced by one he had painted. Hanging to the left was a photo that George Hurrell had taken of the two of us. I was in profile with my hair cascading over his shoulders. He was facing the camera. That is the photo he liked best and the one he practiced strengthening his eyesight on.

Near the foot of his bed was a large white desk facing the wall, adorned with photos of all his good friends, like Joe Gray, Alfred Perles, Lawrence Durrell, and a gorgeous color photograph of Lisa Lu. There were also several pictures of his times in Big Sur.

On the opposite wall was a shelf of some of his favorite books, many of which were now out of print. Next to that a trunk that reminded me of a pirate's treasure chest held the letters, photos, and gifts that I had given him. Looking out the window of his bedroom one could see exotic flowers and lush plants and overgrown trees around his Olympic-sized pool.

There was one large room, also overlooking the pool, that served as his painting room. Paints, brushes, and pad were neatly arranged on a ping-pong table.

In the living room, the furniture was sparse, consisting of a couple of chairs and ottomans; there were also a television and one of the largest stone fireplaces I had ever seen. He enjoyed sitting in front of the fire and smelling the aroma of the burning wood.

The kitchen area consisted of a large table and chairs surrounded by cheerful and bright watercolors either he had painted or friends had given him.

There is something of a landmark in his house . . . the bathroom. The first time I saw that famous bathroom was in a documentary on Henry. I was amazed then and even more so when Henry took me on a tour. Pasted on all the walls were pictures of dozens of people from his past. There were some of his dear friend Blaise Cendrars; there were many nude photographs of beautiful women; some movie stars and some ordinary everyday women. Also, seeming to watch whoever was in the little room, was a photo of an Indian guru with legs folded in the Lotus position.

His children, Tony and Val, lived upstairs as well as whomever was looking after Henry and the household at the time.

The front rooms of the house were rarely ever used, except the living room, which served as an office for his secretary a few days a week. But in every room there were books, lots of books. And a great many of these were books Henry had written, now in a multitude of foreign translations.

●

Sunday—July 10, 1976

Dear Brenda—

Tried phoning you around noon today but the line was busy. Thought it best not to bother you on your day off.

But I can't resist writing you again. Do you mind? Your image floats before me continually. I find myself talking to your "astral" self! Perhaps it's all rubbish, but I think not!

I just finished reading a wonderful book about Walt Whitman, who is my favorite American. What things I learned. Especially about friendship and love. All my life I have been blessed with good warm friends, so much so that my women became quite jealous of them. It is ironic, isn't it, that a woman's greatest rival may be her man's best friend, not another woman!

I imagine you to have many women friends as well as men friends. And I mean friends, not lovers. You seem like a complete woman. I don't even imagine you to be jealous.

Tonight one of Val's actress friends will cook dinner for me. (I wish it were you instead.) Anyway, she's a great talker and it's always enjoyable seeing her.

Tuesday night the Persian lady will cook for me. She comes on strong!

Brenda, I guess I'm rather empty-headed today. Forgive me for this wan, weak missive. I hope tomorrow I will see word from you. I always look through all the envelopes first in search of one from you. I have the fever or the itch, whatever you call it.

I still picture you sitting on the kitchen sink and never worried about getting your dress wet. I also remember how you smiled at the waitress in the Gardens. There's something regal and hoydenish (too) about you.

Bless you!

HENRY

July 15, 1976

My lovely Brenda—

I have returned from the Press Club luncheon and am starved. The meal was a strange American sort of one. No wine—just coffee and tea with the food. After a cup of soup came a salad (which I didn't eat) and then a piece of cake. That's all! I kept expecting another course but it never came. However, it was a good reception I received. They kept firing questions at me and laughed a great deal—so I must have hit it off well with them. They were all correspondents for foreign papers. No Americans, thank God!

I came back and took a little snooze, during which time my mind kept reverting to that erotic-porno Japanese film I told you about. When it is released to local theatres, would you care to see it with me? I would value a woman's opinion, especially someone who is in the films, who is not prudish or squeamish and who has a critical faculty.

Now I want to say a few words about the batch of photos. They are lying beside me and the one on top which you call your "ultra Hollywood" pic is to my mind extremely beautiful and seductive—due perhaps to the way your thick mass of hair drapes itself about your head. But the look in your eyes is exciting. Next up is the one in a bikini at 4:00 A.M. God, but you look ravishing. Excuse me for putting it this way, but I can't help it. You look like you are ready to be laid. Though you didn't do it deliberately, I am sure, yet your pelvis juts forth most invitingly. And those thighs of yours! Made to crush a man's ribs!

Shall I go on? (I hear you say Yes!) Next up is the girl with the straw hat. Reminds me of a famous painting by Matisse. The design on brim of hat is very intriguing—as pattern.

Next I have nothing to say about—you say on back "Thinking of someone I loved far away." A faint reminder of Laurette Taylor, ever hear of her?

The next—with Russian dancer is like from Ravel's "Bolero"—*non?* I feel jealous of him. Nor do I understand what you are trying to tell me about your present lover, Dan. One little detail . . . I notice that even with your shoulder straps slipping off to your arms, your breasts do not pop out! What control! Or is it carefully studied?

And now we come to the one you refer to as "crude." In another woman it might be so considered but not with you! Your look is wonderful. Naturally one's eye travels immediately to the crotch; one also can't help noticing that you reveal more than usual of the one teat— right? Brenda, it is possibly what one might call a lascivious pose, but with a body like yours, anything is forgiven. Besides, aren't you the girl who wrote me that her whole body was one big erogenous zone? Didn't you also tell me that my so-called obscene books were not obscene but natural? You know, it's strange, but as I was opening the envelope of photos I said to myself—"I'll bet this time she sends me some sexy ones!" I'm surprised at you using the word "crude." It's not crudity but audacity. (Thank you for writing on the backs of them.)

The next one is a misnomer—"rather dull" you wrote on back. Anything but, I'd say. This is virtually an "invitation to the dance," to put it elegantly. Do they really wear swim suits like this—and where—in Italy or La Riviera? I haven't seen any like it in this part of the world. It's very lascivious. And your holding your hand as you do increases the awareness of what we are missing. One says to himself, "Why did they stop at the belly button? Why not cut it a few inches lower and give us the whole show?" (Do I offend you—I hope not.)

And now the last one—the one you like. I agree with you. Your pose is almost that of an Eleanora Duse, my great favorite as actress. She and Garbo—*c'est tout*. Jesus, but I'm hungry, and not just for food. I may put your photos under my pillow tonight in order to summon the dreams I desire. Do you mind? Brenda, your letters make me more and more "delirious"—I think that's the word for it. What erogenous zones I have left are quivering with hopeless anticipation. Nothing in the world could give me a greater thrill than to take you (roundabout expression) or even just feel your secret parts. You are treating an old man like me royally. Like a prince, I might say. But each letter, each photo, only increases his (base) appetites. You can appreciate that, can't you?

I am talking rather boldly this time, but not without encouragement, I feel. After all, think of it as one erogenous zone talking radar to another. I'm sure we speak the same language, only using different words. Am I not right?

Brenda, I must stop or else . . . To know anything about your horoscope one must have place of birth and the hour you were born. Can you furnish these? Then I'll see what Omarr, my astrologer friend, has to say. Though he has multiple sclerosis he has (4) women on his string, usually on the end of his cock!

HENRY

Same day—later—July 18, 1976

Brenda, my delight!

I tried to get you on the phone a few minutes ago but don't know whether I got the answering service or just ether waves. So I hung up.

But you're still with me, like a foetus in the womb (only I'm missing the womb).

It's been on my mind to ask you if you ever read any of these famous love stories:

1) Tristan and Isolde
2) Abelard and Heloise
3) Laura and Petrarch

As for Orpheus and Eurydice, enclosed is what my secretary found in the Encyclopedia. Not much, sorry to say. You seem to think I'm a great scholar—but I'm not. I've read a great deal, but never in scholarly fashion.

Two authors I wonder if you ever read—1) Dostoievsky, 2) Isaac B. Singer? Or, and my perennial favorite—Knut Hamsun, author of *Hunger*, *Victoria*, and *Mysteries*, among others. Have you? I love the way he handles love. *Mysteries* is my great favorite. Have read it 6 or 8 times and would read it again tomorrow if someone put it in my hands. If you'd like to try it, I'll hunt up a copy for you. He's long out of print, I'm afraid. If it's true, as Omarr says, that Scorpio becomes the characters she reads about, then I too am a Scorpio. I go nuts reading *Mysteries* yet my children, who read well, don't care for it. Knut Hamsun is my favorite author, though Dostoievsky is the greater writer. (Do you know his famous woman character—Filipovna—in *The Idiot*?)

Well, tonight I seem to be on cooler ground, don't I though? It's only a foil or mask. Underneath I'm still smoldering for this Venus woman. By the way, I mailed you a copy of Omarr's little book on Scorpio for 1976. See where I turned the page down. I know Scorpio by heart. I wonder where your Venus, Moon, and Mars are? Will tell a lot. Do you know the aria in Wagner's *Tristan and Isolde*? Do you know the opera was almost censored and banned? The music is sexual. It does get to your blood, no question about it. Just one prolonged "fragrant delectus." I mean the "Liebestod" part. In other words—an everlasting orgasm. But you probably know all about it . . .

Tell me, how did you hit it off with Coppola? Is he re-hiring you? Jesus, but I'm asking a lot of questions tonight. Pardon me! I sound like a professor. But it's only that I like to share certain good, beautiful things with you. Savvy?

Did you ever see that soft porno called *Emmanuelle?* Did you like it? I'm curious. Enough of questions. I am hungry still for more letters and more photos. I love the way you utilize your time, writing me at odd moments in odd places. Great! Few women seem able to do that. But I keep forgetting that you are not an ordinary woman, you are Brenda, the volcano, the *con furiosa, toujours prête à bruler tout ce qu'elle touche* (meaning—always ready to set afire whatever she touches).

I hope I can go to sleep. Last night I awoke, slept out, at 1:30 A.M. Had a notion to call you, as you once suggested, but didn't want to give you a sleepless night.

You mentioned the moon being in Capricorn the last few days. That explains my rather torrid letters, no?

Brenda, I press you tight and kiss you avidly a thousand times. (Give me more strength, O Lord!)

HENRY

•

Henry felt he was clairvoyant and psychic. He would predict certain happenings, some of which eventually came true. He was fascinated by astrology, astronomy, and numerology as well. Sometimes he would send me his psychic readings.

•

Same day—a little later

Beloved—

Do I dwell too much on your beautiful body? Don't forget that it's you who inspire this adoration.

I feel I must express a few thoughts about your mind and your soul, for God has also richly endowed you in these areas too. I think first of all of your voice, the pitch and the tonality. They never vary, good weather or bad, which means you are harmoniously equilibrated—at least in public or in my presence. If you have emotional fits you don't show them. It's always a bell-like clarity to your voice. It also has a joyous ring, or rather a tinkle. You think with your whole organism, including your private parts, maybe particularly with these parts. It lends color to everything you do or say, even to a gesture. Am I making you too perfect? No, only as I see you through my worshipful gaze. Your soul is utterly mysterious—but it is intact and generous and understanding. If it can hate it can also forgive. It is abiding, like the Rock of Ages. It does not change color, like the chameleon. There is something leonine about it. You are a Scorpio that is non-poisonous. One can keep you as a pet without fear. You can swim in troubled waters and be at peace. You radiate peace and good will. Your sexual fantasies are inherited and spring from the heart rather than the vulva. Your purity is the outcome of your vitality, which was God-given. You have a streak of Semiramis in you, but it will disappear as your love deepens.

That's all I can tell you this evening. Be with me Thursday—in fine fettle.

Your adoring

HENRY

•

One morning I phoned Henry and asked if I could drop by in the late afternoon around four-thirty and give him a hug and say hello, and he answered yes, but he would be leaving the house at six for dinner. He greeted me at the door, as he often did when he was in good spirits, and I gave him his promised hug and kiss and we shuffled into his bedroom to talk for about an hour nonstop. Then we went into the living area so he could show me the new paintings he did that day, when the doorbell rang. He got this mischievous look on his face and said, "Brenda, quick, hide behind the draperies. It's Lisa Lu and I haven't broken the news to her about you. She will be very jealous if she sees you here." So he guided me behind the drapes and neatly patted the folds where my body was bulging, to make it look as if no one was there. But my feet were sticking out and there was nothing to do about that because the drapes were a bit short.

He told me to be perfectly still because he would be in a lot of trouble if I was seen. I said, "Okay, I'll just hold my breath." "No," he retorted, "don't do that. You might faint."

In the foyer, before he opened the door, he whispered, "Brenda, are you all right?" I said, "Sure, but try and hurry because this is not very comfortable."

I could hear him giggle before he opened the door as if he was really pulling a fast one. He greeted Lisa with "Gee, you're a little early, aren't you? You wait here, I have to go and get my coat." Lisa said, "But your coat closet is right here in front of you."

Henry didn't miss a beat. "I guess I'm a little bit excited, I was waiting for you so anxiously. Forgive me, I'll just turn off the lights in the ping-pong room. Must save electricity, you know."

With a twinkle in his eye, he hurried back to tell me we narrowly escaped a messy situation and that everything worked out fine. "She didn't suspect a thing."

I remembered that he had been in a similar situation with Anaïs Nin, only he was the one who had to hide behind the drapery.

In an earlier letter Henry had stated that he had at least six women "on my string." I feel that all these pretty women gave him a reason to live, to wake up each morning, because he could believe he was still the Romeo of yesteryear. As long as he could fantasize, he could shrug off the aches and pains.

•

July 21, 1976

My dear, dear Brenda—

Yes, I do write to a lot of women as well as men, my correspondence is enormous and covers the whole globe. But, don't misunderstand—I don't write all the women as I do you. I do have a rather warm (very friendly) correspondence with a beautiful Japanese in San Francisco and a quite young Korean girl (a genius of a pianist) who may possibly be in love with me. But, my dear Brenda, I couldn't possibly keep a string of beauties—like a stable of fillies. It isn't humanly possible. I don't even desire it. Some publisher who is a great fan of mine and makes me many gifts of art books, wrote in his memoirs of finally meeting me— good description of dialogue—and then ended the passage by saying: "At 82, H.M. still wants to fuck every woman he meets." And that's not true either. There are so many women who bore me to death. Maybe the Women's Libbers think the same way about me but they have never recognized the fact that I love women taken as a whole. And why not? But I can't love them all in the same way. And Brenda, please believe me, you are something very very special to me. . . . I don't know if that was good to give Coppola all those wonderful compliments about me. It will probably leak out. If reporters ever got wise to our goings-on they would ridicule me to death!

How have I forgotten to tell you about Coppola—or didn't I? He never showed up. Had to meet Marlon Brando before taking the plane back to Philippines. Seems Brando is dissatisfied with script!

To come back to Francis, I'm sure he would like to have you in his stable, assuming he has one. That's why he was so shy. (Men too are shy sometimes, you know, or "innocent," like me. Ho ho!)

You say "the great lovers" is one of your favorite topics. Not your lovers, I hope. You mean Garbo and the like? It's mine too. That and "unrequited" love.

When you finish reading the books I bring tomorrow I will have more for you—if you have the stomach for it. For example: I have the book about Walt Whitman, the *Tale of Tristan and Isolde*, *Against the Grain* by Huysmans (Oscar Wilde called it his Bible of Aesthetics). It's up to you how much you can absorb. If I said "take" it would sound like *Deep Throat* and the Sword Swallower biz, eh what?

So you enjoy my sensual writing too! Do you realize you are guilty of euphemism frequently? That is, not saying exactly what you mean. Beating around the bush.

And, as for nudity, don't you go about your own home naked sometimes? Did you know that Benjamin Franklin used to do it and recommended it to all good Americans. It makes one relax, feel free, is good for skin and circulation, and gets one to appreciate one's own body. From doing that to posing for a painter is but a step. Naturally I am not thinking of porno films, whether soft or hard. But your body is a gift to the world! Make it known. When the young woman who posed for Botticelli's "Venus Rising from the Sea" died at an early age, people went mad, flung themselves at her coffin, wept and howled. You too are a Venus—*en chair et os*, as the French say—meaning "in the flesh."

Do I sound "Hedonistic"? How can I help it with you? You invite romantic dreams, "the skin one loves to touch," nocturnal emissions and God knows what all.

Love yourself! As you would expect others to love you.

Ta ta now!

HENRY

·

Henry was intrigued that I was part Indian, and said we ought to become blood brothers. I thought it was a touching idea, and before I knew it Henry had me cleaning a penknife with alcohol. I went first, pricking myself on the wrist. (I still have a tiny scar there.) Henry took the knife and went a little overboard. We managed to exchange blood and vows to love each other forever when I began to realize that his wrist wasn't drying up. I rushed to get a towel to wrap him with, and every time I checked it there was fresh blood. I was on the verge of calling the paramedics when it finally began to slow down. Henry thought the whole thing extremely romantic.

Soon afterward, Henry came to my house for dinner. Henry had been feeling melancholy, as he would say, so I planned to give him a special present to try to lift his spirits. First, I told him in detail some things I had learned about Captain John Smith and Pocahontas that had always had a special interest for me. She had really been the first woman diplomat, representing the New World in London. When she was still a young girl she had given John Smith, whose life she had saved many times, a small vial with her blood in it to wear around his neck, hanging by a necklace she had woven from her own long black hair. She told him it was the greatest gift she could give him to show her love. It was her "heart's blood."

Now, in my family on my mother's side, we also have a special gift. The firstborn of each generation is given a family treasure, a six-carat ruby, which is placed on his forehead at birth and is meant to give the child special powers. I had been the lucky recipient in my family and it was intended to go to my firstborn. But since I had no children and no immediate plans to marry, I decided to break tradition and after telling Henry the Pocahontas story, I gave him the ruby.

He loved his present, and from then on whenever he went out he wore it around his neck. At night it was always by his bedside. Some weeks after he received my gift, he presented me with a coin which he had worn for many years. He told me the story of this gift, that centuries ago the coin had been found in a sunken treasure chest, and had then been worn by St. Francis of Assisi.

My mother, by the way, did not speak to me for six months.

•

July 23, 1976

My darling Brenda—

Last night I went to bed in a state of bliss. What a wonderful evening you gave me! Thank you, thank you! (And here are a few hundred kisses in the interim.)

I can't get over how beautiful your little home is. Like you in every way. Too bad there were no portraits of you by Bonnard, Renoir, Dubuffet, Braque, or Picasso. Only sit for the Masters! Only sleep with the Masters! Eat and drink with the nobodies or the somebodies, but no more.

When you came out with the cookies in the white robe I was astonished. What an actress you are. But most of all I remember the tender looks you gave me, the warm hug, the shower of kisses.

One funny little incident sticks in my crop. When you escorted me to the bathroom and then stood there, as if expecting me to ask you to hold me up. I'm sure you would have done just that had I requested it! What a woman!

And then that story about Olivier. Utterly fantastic. Great! Like that one day some director is going to seize on you, make you his star, and let you be known to all the world.

Oh, yes, and the Pocahontas yarn. Captain John Smith burned— and her attitude. How noble some women can be! What a shame they can't tell us the naked truth in history books.

I seem chock full of wonderful memories of last night—tidbits to perfume my sleep. Bliss, bliss—no doubt about it. The blood-brother to ecstasy. But more steady, more lasting. I'll cherish your heart's blood. Have put it somewhere for safe keeping.

Well, I imagine you are winging your way to Utah and to Dan. It's great that you have room in your heart for the two of us. Or am I being a bit presumptuous?

What a shiver of delight went through me as you kissed me good night.

I'm going to stop now in order to do some work, but don't know if you will let me. You keep tugging at my heart. It's almost as if we had drunk some witch's brew! (Tristan and Isolde.)

More anon. Take good care of yourself. Don't get exhausted from love or work!

HENRY

Dear Brenda—

You know those black holes in the sky which are such mysteries to astronomers? Well, I feel as if there were a black hole in my private sky since you left.

I was asleep and Val woke me to sign a few prints which she just sold to some movie director. (She loves to make money, Val. So does Tony. I never had that bug.)

Anyway, since I was up I decided to stay up and chin with you a while. What about? Anything and everything. Your chaste walls, for example; your spotless refrigerator and the fleurs de lys pattern on Sarah Bernhardt's blouse as I was taking a leak *chez vous*. And those lovely portraits of you—Hurrah! That body, that face, that *je ne sais quoi* (don't know what)—all enough to drive a man out of his mind.

When I first heard you say "my period" I was almost shocked. What! The shy Brenda telling me about her period, her profuse bleeding, her painful spasms! Incredible. But how natural you were!

And then in the bathroom waiting hesitantly, ready, I do believe, to take it out and hold it for me, if necessary. That didn't shock me; that merely told me how considerate you could be—and still remain shy! I think such behavior one might expect of a Japanese woman, not an American.

Funny you telling me of Captain John Smith's burnt penis and I sending you the review of Japanese film in which the woman cuts off the dead man's penis. Did you understand why she tried to strangle him while mounting him? Did you know there is a legend about the hanging of a man, that the moment his neck snaps and with it his cortex he ejaculates automatically. And where there is a gallows there grows a plant called mandrake or mandragora, shaped like a human head, born of the semen of a hanged man! There was a German novel built around this theme called *Alraune* by Hans-Heinz Emers—many years ago.

Do you own a copy of *Tristan and Isolde*? If not, I'd like to send you one. This and Emily Bronte's *Wuthering Heights* are two very passionate tales, no holds barred. Tell me, with all your other talents, do you also write—stories, plays, scripts? You put in such a full day that I wonder if you can find time for such a pastime or even for making love.

From the little hints you have dropped about your love life I imagine it to be full and rich. I also think of it as rather paradoxical—i.e., extreme passion together with great modesty. If it weren't for the latter element, you would be in danger of being a nymphomaniac! Right?

You said at dinner table, "Everybody has a birthmark." But that's not so. Vaccination marks, *oui!* But not birthmarks. I think if you will examine yourself more closely you will discover yet another birthmark and this time in the vicinity of the pussy willow (maybe hidden by the pubic hair). The Japanese sometimes say "public hair."

Now I am treading on dangerous ground, aren't I? But I do so only with your kind permission and not to deny you a single crumb!

How I long to see your next letter! I hope it's a good "torrid" one. Did you notice that the subtitle for the Japanese film was "the corrida of love?" A *corrida* for me, eh?

HENRY

Same day—still later!

Brenda, I wish God had given me the gift of writing about sex like D. H. Lawrence. Somehow my efforts always seem crude and shocking, even to liberal-minded individuals.

Why do I speak thus?

Because, willy nilly we are approaching that delicate yet most powerful region called the genitals. Just as Walt Whitman felt compelled to include in his *Leaves of Grass* the "Songs of Adam," which alienated so many of his admirers here and abroad, so I feel I run the great risk of alienating your affection once I begin to plunge in where angels fear to tread.

Yet, do I not have a collaborator? Have you not kept pace with me step by step all along the way? Do you not write screaming messages between the lines, so to speak? Do you not encourage me to be myself?

Before I go any further, let me tell you of a little incident some few years ago in Paris, after the publication in French of *Sexus*. All of a sudden the French authorities decided that they would take no more of my nonsense. They threatened me with imprisonment, imagine that!

Fortunately there is a court in France, the like of which we don't have here—a sort of pre-trial court. There I was summoned with my French lawyer. After quite a bit of questioning, the judge leaned over his desk and, gazing at me severely, said, "Monsieur Miller, there is one last question I must put to you. Please pay strict attention." The question was—"Do you honestly believe a writer has the right to say anything he pleases in a book?"

I took a few studied moments before replying and then I said calmly but with conviction, "I do, your honor!" (With that the clerk, who had been taking notes and watching me most attentively throughout, looked in my direction and silently clapped his hands under his little table.)

Now the judge came down from his dais, hugged me, kissed me on each cheek ("the accolade"), and said, "You belong with the immortals: François Villon, Baudelaire, Zola, and Balzac. I salute you!"

I didn't mention that during the course of the proceedings I was so tense that suddenly I wanted to urinate, I felt my bladder would burst. I turned to my lawyer and asked where the lavatory was. To my astonishment, he said, "You can't go. Do it in your pants if you have to." Whereupon I did it and there was a big stream of water across the floor, almost to the judge's feet. I was not tried again nor imprisoned either. I was granted "an amnesty." But from then on I was a hero in French literature, one of their very own. And I am treated like one to this day.

Well, does all this give me the right to speak my mind to you? I am still hesitant. I think I shall wait for your reaction before proceeding further. Have mercy on me! You've taken me to your heart. Now take me other places!

HENRY

•

Henry was unpredictable. One day he would write me erotic, suggestive letters and then the next time we would meet he would apologize profusely and beg my forgiveness if I was the least bit offended. He explained this behavior often by reminding me that he was a man, made of all the various parts a man is made of, and that he must at any and all times be himself. He desperately wanted me to understand this side of him.

Sometimes when he would write asking a sexual favor, or if the entire letter was abrasive, I would not read it. Instead I had a drawer that I put those particular letters in and I would read them at a later time when I could distance myself from them. He would ask repeatedly, did I receive the letter and what did I think? In reply, I would say, yes, I received it but I prefer not to comment now, but I promise that I will later. And, of course, I did when the time was right. I never wanted to hurt or offend Henry. I cared too much for him to be inconsiderate of his feelings.

There were days when I wished he wouldn't talk so much about
my body or pretend he was falling so he could touch my breast
or thigh. He was not a quitter, so it was up to me to find my
sense of humor about that relentless situation.

At one point Henry told me he wanted to write me a *really*
risqué letter and he hoped he wouldn't offend me. If any other
eighty-seven-year-old man had suggested something like this, I
would have been put off—but who was I to tell Henry Miller
what he should or should not write? I told him that if he thought
it was going to be too erotic that he might consider writing the
letter in French.

•

Same day—later 8/7/76

Your lucky day, Brenda! Was it? Spent two hours today talking to a
young couple (fans) from Salt Lake City. After that one solid hour answering Lisa's questions about words and phrases she didn't know—in
the *Book of Friends*.

Answering her questions, I realized very strongly that there is a
man's language and a woman's language—in all countries. The man's
language sounds flippant and derogatory where women and sex is concerned. For instance, consider phrases like—"I'm going to get me a
piece of tail," or "I want my nooky," or "She was a pushover," etc., etc.
In Japanese, though the women may have the same vocabulary as the
men, they pronounce the words more softly, more ingratiatingly.

Maybe that's why you asked me to write the erotic letter in French. If
the French do use "dirty" language, they make it sound humorous, too.

In Chinese I find there is no equivalent for the words and phrases I
use. Chinese must be a rather dull, flat-sounding (not writing!) language. Everything too explanatory. Very few metaphors. Yet they have
good poetry!!

Did you like the printed words on the flap of my big envelope? I
hope they didn't irritate you. So many American women I know bristle
when I mention the Japanese woman! Jealousy, envy—what? You
could well pass for an Oriental of some description—Hindu, rather
than Chinese or Japanese!

By now, from dint of thinking about it so much, I can virtually
visualize the "campy" photo at the Post Office. You are still wearing a

"seventh veil" only it is shorter, more revealing. Your teats are exposed, but in a discreet way. There is a cricket hopping from your left leg to your right leg, then losing himself in your silver dollar navel. *Vous êtes intriguée mais assez triste. Vous avez besoin d'un homme.*

Assez pour ce soir.

HENRY

(IN FRENCH FOR BRENDA)

The idea which you suggested to me is so audacious that I am not sure of being capable of doing what you asked of me. Since I have known you you have occupied my thoughts perpetually. In my fantasies I have done all sorts of things with you. I have guarded in my head the idea not to offend you. At the same time thru your letters I can sense that I may dare to do and say much more than I actually am doing. Your body itself is an invitation to do everything.

The scene that comes to mind repeats itself often. I am at your house looking at your paintings. You immediately give me something to drink. The drink rises to our heads. You are dressed in a very thin and transparent skirt. Above your belly-button you are wearing nothing. Your breasts are splendid. You have the appearance of a dancer. (Something from Degas.) Your legs are strong and beautiful. All of a sudden I throw myself on you, and lift your skirt. You are totally naked under the skirt. Your little puss with black and copious hair makes me immediately tighten up. I plunge my hand between your thighs and I see that you are already wet. You seem very excited, ready to do anything. That is not surprising. I know you from centuries, what I mean to say is from other incarnations. We were lovers many times. Sometimes you were a prostitute at the temple—in the Indies, in Egypt and in other countries. You are always a lady of pleasure, but always religious. Your religion was always "sex"—just like the practitioners of Tantra of today. You teach the young, the men and the women. For you it is a question of art. That's why you now appear to be an expert.

Without the slightest blush you lightly touch your cunt with your right hand. Then . . . with two fingers of each hand you open the crack between your legs, and you show me the small lips that tremble like a little bird. The juice flows liberally; your thighs gleam.

Without saying a word you put your hand in my trouser and catch my flute (or the bollard if you prefer). Your hands so strong but delicate, play with it as if it were a musical instrument. You are choked up and irresistible. I want to "play" immediately, and most of all when you put your tongue in my mouth. From there your mouth turns to suck my flute gently. It is difficult to remain standing. Luckily the couch is on your side. We fall onto the couch together, mouth on mouth and flute on cunt. I have not yet penetrated you. How warm you are! You give me kisses all over. I want to kiss you. You are totally ready. You press on my flute and put it between your legs. I enter softly, even slowly. Your organ is deliciously formed. It is narrow and deep. You hold me as one would a finger. Naturally I cannot retain myself anymore. I come—as do you—at the same time.

We remain like that for a while intertwined like serpents. I want to tear myself away but you do not allow me to. You hold me with strong muscles. After some time I feel movement inside of you. Little by little I begin to swell. Now you lift your legs and put them over my shoulders. You are totally open and wet. You do not stop coming. Your eyes turn towards the ceiling. You ask me to continue, to do more. You say [in English], "Fuck me, Henry, fuck me! Shove it in to the hilt. I'm so horny." It is the first time that you have used such language with me. It drives me wild. "God give me the power, the strength," I say to myself, "and I will kiss you endlessly." Do not forget that I am relating to you a fantasy. I do not understand where the power comes from to give you pleasure for so long.

You are insatiable. You make all sorts of movements, sometimes gestures that are completely delirious and obscene. You have lost your mind. You are totally sex and nothing else. Knowing that you can kill me you detach yourself from me so that I may breathe. But you do not stop caressing, especially with your tongue. And your body continues to undulate over me. You kiss me like a madwoman!

Et puis quoi? Quelle position? C'est moi qui propose que nous faisons l'amour comme les chiens . . .

•

Henry and I were talking about parenthood, and about what parents contributed to the nature of their children, both good and bad. Henry began to talk about his mother, and he was overcome with anger. His face turned red, and he complained of pains from his heart as he reiterated the injustices he had suffered from her when he was a child. I suggested to him that the time had finally come to forgive her, to make peace with her. We agreed that he couldn't get into heaven if he continued to harbor this hatred.

●

Saturday—8/14/76

Dear Brenda—

I just finished writing about China for a Chinese magazine and another (short) piece on Hokusai for an exposition of his *shunga* (erotic) wood blocks done at the age of 80. The exposition to take place in Paris at "L'Espace Cardin." Erica Jong came for lunch and left only about an hour or so ago. She'd like to find a house in California. After New York, California seems like a Paradise.

I have been thinking of you ever since you put me away early. You went to acting class afterwards, didn't you? You could have told me and left even earlier had you wanted to. I would not have objected.

I notice you observe the other night that I always have "sex" on my mind. Not always, dear Brenda. There are a thousand other things more important to me than sex. But when I come across a creature who is all sex I can't help but betray my feelings.

A lapse of a few hours here. I was in bed but got up to finish this. I want to make mention to you once again of one of my favorite writers— Marie Corelli.

I rediscovered her about a year ago. I now have ten of her titles. Here are the names of some I read:

1.) *A Romance of Two Worlds*
2.) *The Sorrows of Satan*
3.) *The Soul of Lilith*
4.) *The Life Everlasting.*

She lived in the latter part of the 19th century, during the Victorian epoch. She never speaks of sex, never mentions any sexual organ or any intercourse. Yet she is a thrilling, inspiring writer—for men and women. (I don't think you would like her, though.)

When I was waking up a few minutes ago, I found myself writing in my head. The strangest thing—I was dead and had just realized that I was in Devachan (the realm between death and rebirth). My mother is coming toward me looking radiant. She seems very young. "O Henry," she begins, "I have waited for you so long. What kept you on earth all this time?"

(This is the first time I hear my mother murmur endearing words.) I am choked with emotion. "Mother . . ." is all I can say. And then I discover that the tears are running down my cheeks.

You know, I believe that I hated my mother all my life, to the very end. I wonder what this dream signifies—that I am approaching death or that I am losing all hatred, all bitterness?

As I got out of bed I wondered if I should try to write a short book on Mother and Son in the Afterworld?? Very strange for me. Your talk must have done something to me deep down, softened me up in some strange, inexplicable way.

Did you ever read my essay on The Womb? Very surrealistic. I love the thought of the womb—so cosy, so nourishing.

Enuf now—I'm sleepy. Love

HENRY

•

Henry's daily routine was basically the same, with a slight variation depending on how strong he felt.

He usually would greet the morning around seven-thirty to eight o'clock and would either call and say good morning, or he would just lie in bed and listen to the birds chirping and the different sounds that one might hear at that hour.

At 9:00 Charles, his nurse, would arrive and prepare him for the day. This consisted of washing, exercising, a little cheerful conversation, vitamins, and breakfast. He adored Charles for a number of reasons. They had one basic characteristic in common—they both loved life and they laughed a lot. Sometimes I would drive over early for a swim and a run around the Palisades, returning to find Charles' big black Cadillac parked in front of the house. It always made me feel good to know that Charles was there.

After breakfast Henry went through his mail and answered as many fan letters as possible. Letters he felt were exceptionally good, he would send on to me to enjoy. If he was working on a new book or an article, this would be the time he would take to work. If not, he would sit at his ping-pong table and do a watercolor or two, depending on how good he felt. After working a few hours, he would take lunch and after, a little nap. He would often have visitors. Some were good friends, others came to ask for favors. Can you lend me money, would you teach me to write, can I live at your house for a while? I'm doing a film, would you please be in it? Sometimes Henry was easily accessible and other times it would be impossible to see him.

When I met Henry he told me he hated the telephone and would seldom use it because he couldn't hear very well. But as time went on and we knew each other better, he called at least once a day. He would leave long messages on my answering machine, taking into consideration that he was always teaching me. There would be a story he forgot to tell me or some valuable information he forgot to write. I often called him after I got into bed just to say good night and send him my love.

•

Sept. 4, 1976

Chérie—

All day, I've been wanting to write you, getting my mind readied for it, and then at 3:00 P.M. comes a neighbor (from Arkansas) and buys $130.00 worth of my books—but takes up 2 hours doing it. Fuck her!

Any way, *mon chou*, how goes it today? No letter from you and I suppose you won't get my Special Delivery till Saturday—and this one only next Tuesday! Wow! We are really fucked up by the holiday, eh? Those post office bastards ought to work night and day and Sundays and holidays, too.

Tomorrow I'm sure I'll receive the letter you mailed yesterday. It better be good! I'm counting on it.

You know, I was studying that photo of you and the boy. It's amazing how beautiful you look as a man. Without losing a milligram of femininity you have developed a nice streak of masculinity. It adds to your charm, not detracts. You are such a candid, frank person. I'm sure if I asked you seriously to describe your cunt (physically) you would do

it like an expert. How many things you have told me about yourself—
intimate things! Women don't usually do that. Not right off leastways.

Am I falling into a Southern way of talking? If so, attribute it to your
influence. You can't make me do things but you influence me a great
deal.

I love to tell inquisitive people that I'm in love with a young woman
from Mississippi. I wouldn't say Hattiesburg, but I feel when I say Mississippi they immediately connect up with Mark Twain and those big
two-wheeler boats.

I'm running off the track. This is all bosh what I'm writing you. I
had very definite things to say but they have been blurred by the advent
of that talkative real estate woman who lives on Alma Real nearby. Do
you know that *alma* means a soul in Spanish? Isn't it another coinci-
dence that the next street to Ocampo should be the street of the Soul?
And a few blocks away is the street of the Womb (*La Combre*)!

Strange how with me soul and sex are always united like Castor and
Pollux, the Heavenly Twins.

Yesterday came the woman from Japan. She gave me a gift of a
beautiful, flexible silver paper cutter. Told me a lot about the ungodly
man-woman situation in Japan. The men, as every Japanese woman
tells me, are simply incorrigible. They are weak (caricatural) hangovers
from the days of the Samurai. (Have you read *Shogun* by Clavell?
Seems most everyone is and raving about it. It's out in paperback now.)

By the way, I wrote you "precipitately" when it should be pre-
cipitously, did you notice? There is the noun—precipitate. (Does it
matter?) I'm simply trying to hold you to the paper. It's a way of holding
you in my arms and caressing you.

Did my last letter surprise you a bit? Were we then on the same
wavelength? Or was I way off this time?

Listen, I'm no longer so very horny, but when I rise up in bed and
slide to the edge of the bed my balls get squashed. Can it be that they
are growing now, at my age? If only my prick would follow suit! Sometimes, when it's snoozing, it looks like a lost snail to me. Now that's one
thing about the cunt. The variations throughout the day are not so
conspicuous. Right?

This reminds me of a conversation I had the other night in Malibu
with a lively, delicate French woman. She had been arguing with a
French man about the fact that they always use *con* (cunt) in a derogatory way. When a Frenchman says—"sale con" (dirty cunt) he doesn't
mean that. That's his way of saying "stupid bastard." Anyway, he got
her so riled that finally she retaliated by calling him "sale couille"—
couille means balls. There is no part of man's sexual apparatus which is

ever used in a derogatory way. (Here they resemble the Japanese a bit.)

Did I ever tell you how inventive the Japanese man is when it comes to delineating a woman's cunt? They have all sorts of terminologies for this organ. The cunt they appreciate the most is called "like a thousand earthworms." Another, not so good, is "hit the ceiling," and for a very big cunt it is "falling downstairs." All expressed in a word or two. Remember my water color "Asamara"? Means "morning erection." Morning, mind you, no other time of day.

> *Folle à la messe*
> *Molle à la fesse*
>
> François Villon
>
> (Crazy about mass, soft in the ass.)

Next Tuesday I'll be looking for a Loulou of a letter from you. You'll have a whole week-end to cook something up. Make it a good bouillabaise! And throw in a few *baisers* (noun or verb, no matter.)

Are you slithering around now? You do get restless, don't you? And don't you like to open and close your legs? Doesn't that excite you? In French, by the way, the verb *exciter* means to get passionate—not "exciting." *Alors, attention!*

Have you "learned" anything from this letter? Or should I have added something about Virgil, Ovid, Rabelais, Cendrars, Céline, or Octave Mirbeau?

My eye is getting bleary. Signal to quit. How can I? You have me in your grip, just as sure as if your thighs and mine were interlocked. You are the acme (apotheosis) of sex, yet cool as a cucumber outwardly. You are North and South in one. You are the monsoon and the deluge all in one. You are you—and that's saying a lot. So long for a while. (I may write more—later.)

HENRY

Same Day

Dear Brenda—

This is my third and last letter to you today. Just to tell you about one new photo of you, the head only. Your hair looks as if you had just come out of the water. The expression in your eyes is the most soulful of all. Christ, but you are beautiful! Ravishingly so. Were you looking at your lover when this picture was taken? Your mouth is always like a bow—full, sensual, lips to kiss, to bite, to glue oneself to.

You are drugging me with these photos. Even when I was very young and very romantic, I never gazed at a girl's photo with the passion that I gaze at you!! In this one with the hair slightly disarranged your expression beats that of Greta Garbo—and she was something to look at in her day.

You will remain beautiful all your life, I feel. Like Botticelli's Venus, you rose from the sea and are still all foam!

Good night now!

HENRY

•

There were a few regular cooks in the Miller household. Val, his daughter, and Tony, his son, would always cook when they stayed over. His dear friend Sava cooked once a week, as did Bill Pickerall who took good care of Henry and maintained the house. Barbara Kraft, a writer friend of Henry's, also cooked his meals on a regular basis. Barbara was pretty, a great conversationalist as well as a great cook, so she was definitely a favorite.

There was also a string of young girls, usually students or actresses or would-be writers, who had found a path to Henry, and to whom he granted the opportunity to cook for him and join him for a meal. The turnover of these volunteers was pretty fierce because Henry's presence made them nervous. Sometimes he would simply roll his wheelchair into the kitchen and, if the guest chef was interesting or exceptionally attractive, engage her in conversation.

But at dinner if the food wasn't well-made, Henry would tactfully tell them the meal just wasn't to his taste, and that would be the end of that cook.

On Thursdays I usually took him to his favorite restaurant, the Imperial Gardens, a great old Japanese restaurant high in the Hollywood Hills. Henry was friends with the owners, Lyle and

Kinu, loved sushi and sashimi, and spoke a little Japanese. But
if it was raining, I would bring over a hot Italian or French meal
that I prepared at home, or I would cook whatever he had in
the house. He especially liked my making breakfast at night for
him because I made eggs and waffles with a special Canadian
maple syrup.

Once in a while he requested my Southern-fried chicken. He
would sit in his wheelchair and talk to me while I cooked.
Once when I was sitting on the counter and sipping Pernod
with him, we became so wrapped up in our conversation that I
forgot I was cooking. We ended up eating scrambled eggs and
having his favorite dessert—vanilla Häagen-Dazs.

There were times Henry would call and say, 'Brenda, I don't
have a cook tonight. And if you can cook what's here, I'll open
a bottle of the Mersault.' I never refused, even if I was getting
ready to go out to a dinner party with my boyfriend. I would
drive over in my evening dress, cook his meal, drink a little
wine, and catch up with my boyfriend later.

•

8/19/76

Dear Brenda—

I hope you go to class tonight and get the letter I sent there for you.
Here's another . . .

The other day, Charles, my nurse, said to my surprise, "I think I've
got to get me a woman. Come this time of year I wake up too early."
What I wanted to say was, "What you need, Charles, is a foot-warmer."

Anyway, this got me to thinking about a Chinese healer who wrote
me a couple of months ago that he is taking the liberty of giving me a
little advice about old age. Said I ought to go with a woman at least six
or eight times a day. Not ejaculate but go through all the motions of
making love. Like that I might live to be 100. At first I thought he was a
nut but after a time I saw the point of it. Of course you have to be well
off and be your own boss before you can try it.

How does this idea strike you? Tonight at dinner Charles begins
talking about all the women he knows—colored and white. Asks me if
when I'm in love I believe in sharing the woman with other men.

When I said no, he said, "I agree with you." All the time I try to replace women by men—but maybe he's bisexual. He tells me a lot about colored men and women. They sure seem very much like white people in their behavior, don't you think?

Here I am on sex again. Hope you don't mind. . . . One night I may come to the class and watch you all perform. Would that be O.K.?

Now I'm going to bed. My eye won't stand much more writing.

I wish you could read what I'm writing about my mother. You'd get a kick out of it. But first it has to be typed. And I'm not through yet. More tomorrow if possible. I squeeze you, hug you, kiss you, love you—till you suffocate.

                                        HENRY

8/19/76

Dear Brenda—

Not finding any letter from you these last two days is like seeing a deep black hole in a bright blue sky. I haven't written either, not because I didn't hear from you but because I have been overwhelmed with work. (I even had to halt writing that piece about Mother and Son in Limbo.)

Yesterday I gave a young French woman (from the paper Le Monde) a 3-hour interview—it was a cracker jack of an interview! She was the best female ever interviewed me—spoke perfect English and Russian! She is a feminist, works for French Woman's Liberation. Said the American man doesn't look you in the eye. Asked if I could explain the paradox of utter sexual freedom (here) and the same Puritan strain as always. Told me there is a prostitute's union here called Coyote. Each letter stands for something.

The other morning, Brenda, I woke up remembering that it was in Natchez, Miss. I received a wire telling me my father was dying. I took a plane but arrived an hour or so too late. My mother told me that for the last hour that he was alive he was telling the nurses what a wonderful son he had. (I wept when I heard that. I also wept and sobbed like a maniac when I kissed him in the coffin. When I let go I really let go!) Like that, I am afraid to really lose my temper. I could not only kill but I could mutilate my victim. (You'd never think that, would you?) So I have learned patience and forbearance. By the way, I arrived in Natchez from Vicksburg where I had lunch or dinner with some famous Mississippi writer—who?

Dear Brenda, soon as I finish this letter I shall get back to Mamma-Son in the other world. It's a fascinating subject and affords me a catharsis. At the very end I will say to her what I never could say in life, nor she either: "Mother, I love you!"

And does I love my Brenda now, not in the dim hereafter. I'll undoubtedly get there before you. And I'll wait for you. When I talk of Cora, as I did recently, it isn't that I still love her. No, I'm just curious. Yes, we will talk about Dagney and Herr Nagel. I may resemble Nagel in a way, but you don't resemble Dagney, thank God!

HM

Sept. 17, 1976

Dearest Brenda—

A big gap between now and your return. If okay with you I'd like to come to dinner Tuesday night, but if inconvenient for you can make it another night. Incidentally, have you read any of *My Secret Life* yet? Just curious.

You were great last night—in fact all three women were fine, better than the men. I think Oscar is the worst. Shows no emotion in his face—always dead pan. Ann thinks he ought to take mime lessons. So do I. (But how to tell him, eh?)

I wondered why, in the Tennessee Williams play, you kept shaking your head and twirling your mane around like a horse? Was it because of imaginary flies? You were just right for the part and your Southern accent came to the fore in good style. You were also very seductive. One can see what sexual magnetism emanates from you. (The Sicilian comes out strong.)

I got a slight twinge of jealousy when you were saying good night to Peter (the young boyish-looking actor). The way you slung your arm around his neck and kissed him affected me. (Over-sensitive, as usual, I guess) Am probably spoiled by all the attention you shower me with.

Your letter, which I read immediately on coming home, was utterly enchanting. You write like one who has had long practice in writing love letters. There's no hesitation between your feelings and your words. It's quite a gift, you know. Most writers struggle for years to attain it.

You are it, whatever it may be. Also, you are the first woman I have known to combine cunt and intellect—or spirit or soul! I mean it. You are terribly sexy (not just sensual) and at the same time pure as an ethereal being. The name Venus suits you to a T. Venus—Aphrodite. If it had not been Venus it could have been "Juno" (without the peacock).

Talking of cocks, I was taken by surprise when you asked that question at table last night. The only cocks I know of which may take on a little heft are those which do a lot of fucking. Yet a man like George Raft, who made a habit of sleeping with a different woman each night, retained the same cock he had as a teenager—according to my friend Joe Gray who was a good friend of his. Most men with unusually big cocks find themselves in trouble. Prostitutes make them pay double. Ordinary women with ordinary cunts don't want anything to do with those freaks. Yet women will always fantasize about big cocks, *non*? Herriot, one time Prime Minister of France and a most cultured individual, had such an enormous one that he had to strap it to his leg.

For a woman, the supreme thing is to have a rather long, deep one that fits like a glove. And it should be equipped with a thousand earthworms or the equivalent. Some cunts could be called laughing cunts. Others are rather dull, solemn, and dry as a bone.

So you "tend to your own," as you put it. Sounds like you were cultivating a "secret garden." When I think of what your cunt must be like it blows my mind.

To come back to the class . . . you all seem to me to be accomplished actresses. At least you have acquired that wonderful gift of being natural, being oneself. Bravo! Because that's half the battle. Olivier is the actor personified—everything thought out. Burton makes me weep when he recites Shakespeare—because he is Welsh, I think. The Welsh are born poets. I knew Dylan Thomas in London. He wanted me to go back to Wales with him. Offered to let me sleep with his sister. (I believe he slept with her.) There's a lot of incest in Wales—and idiocy and genius—and, my God, what marvelous male voices, what lusty singers and sinners.

Do you ever think any more of Dagney and Herr Nagel in *Mysteries*? I can never forget that line of his when he runs into her in the forest: "Good morning, Froken, is it permitted to touch your puff today?"

Well, my darling Brenda, whether it's permitted or not, I am going to say good night and in doing so I make bold to touch your disarming puff.

Au revoir!

POÈME EN PROSE	**A POEM IN PROSE**
POUR MON VENUS À MOI	**FOR MY VENUS**

Est-ce que vous étiez conscient hier

> Were you conscious last night

Soir du grandeur de la lune?

> Of the grandeur of the moon?

Saviez-vous qu'elle était une livre de miel?

> Did you know that she was a pound of
> honey?

Vous, livre de miel pour tous les couples

> You, oh pound of honey for all the
> couples

accroupis ensemble partout au monde.

> Crouched together everywhere in the
> world.

Les hommes sur le dos avec leurs phallus

> The men on their backs their phalluses

en erection gigantesque.

> in huge erection.

Les femmes avec leurs vagins soupirants

> The women, their vaginas sighing

et fulgurants.

> and flashing.

Tous faisant l'amour comme des

> All making love like

animaux d'enfer.

> animals of hell.

Tous maîtrises par le désir—

> All bridled by the desire—

désir enormement fructueux.

> the incredibly fruitful desire.

L'air etait percé par les sons bizarre—

> The air was pierced by the bizarre
> sounds—

grognements des elephants, le "whimsy" des chevaux, les baas des

> the groaning of elephants, the
> "whinneying" of horses and the bleat-
> ing of

veaux.

calves.

Il serait deplorable si tout n'était

It would be deplorable if everything was

pas commandé par l'ordre du dieu Priapus

not commanded by the God Priapus.

Son empreint fût visible içi et la,

His stamp was visible here and there—

bref, partout.

briefly, everywhere.

Il régnait sur la nuit comme un

He reigned over the night like an

empereur . . . Parfois c'était horrible.

emperor . . . Sometimes it was terrible.

Mais peu à peu l'on entendait la musique Chopinesque, nostalgie,

But little by little one heard the
Chopinesque music, the nostalgia,

sanglots, cris de chameaux—tous

the sobs, the cries of the camels—
everything

très belle.

was very beautiful.

Chopin et Ravel—ajoutez Debussy!

Chopin and Ravel—and also Debussy!

Quelle musique divinie!

Oh what divine music!

Joué par an ange avec le raffinement

Played by an angel with the refinement

d'un prince.

of a prince.

Tout à coup une resurrection.

Suddenly a resurrection.

Les couples assombris se levent et

The obscured couples rise and

commencent a chanter.

begin to sing.

Leurs voix touchent le marge du ciel.

Their voices reach the edge of the sky.

Même les morts sont touchés.

         Even the dead are touched.

Les morts se ravivent, pleins de délire

         The dead are revived, delirious

Maintenant les oiseaux peuvent être

         Now the birds can also

entendu aussi.

         be heard.

"Hark hark the lark at Heaven's gate sings . . . et tra la la."
Oui, les morts et les anges comprennent

         Yes the dead and the angels understand

Anglais—très curieux.

         English—how odd it is.

Les dieux et les demi-dieux parlent

         The gods and the half-gods speak

Hongrois et Polonais

         Hungarian and Polish

Mais seulement entre eux!

         But only amongst themselves!

Arrive l'aube . . . tout devient

         The dawn arrives . . . everything becomes

silencieux. Le monde respire.

         silent. The world breathes.

Les anges disparaissent dans les

         The angels disappear into the

images de Fra Angelico.

         images of Fra Angelico.

Da Vinci dors. Botticelli ouvre ses yeux.

         Da Vinci sleeps. Botticelli opens his eyes.

Le ronde commence sous un

         The world begins under a

Ciel de pâle bleu. Bleuâtre plutot.

         Pale blue sky. Rather bluish.

     Au revoir

         Until we see each other again

             HM

•

Henry said many times to many people that the Nobel Prize was not important to him. His justification for wanting it was that he needed the $160,000 for his children, since taxes would take most of his estate.

I'm not sure that this was the whole story. I would listen to Henry repeat the word "Nobel" when he was referring to the Prize. His eyes would light up and he would be overcome by a rush of excitement. He pronounced "Nobel" as though he were saying "noble." He said it would be a "position of nobility" to have won.

He was told by several astrologers that he would be awarded the highest honor ever presented to a writer. Some psychics and astrologers even told him that the "great event" would be the Nobel Prize.

Every time one of his friends, such as Isaac Singer, received the Prize, they would write to tell him that he should have received it and not them. He liked and respected Singer so much that when that happened, they were both very emotional. By the time Henry was eighty-eight, he felt that his chances of receiving it while still alive were running out.

He encouraged his friends to help the campaign. Isaac Singer wrote a lengthy letter to the Nobel committee, and Lawrence Durrell made numerous phone calls and wrote letters on behalf of Henry. Even Governor Jerry Brown was drawn into helping. I became involved in the campaign, too, writing letters and phoning people I thought might be in a position to help. At one point it seemed as if the whole city was on a crusade to get this award for Henry.

•

10/7/76

Darling Brenda—

No, I'm not dead and I have not forgotten you, only neglected you unwillingly. I have worked like the devil, had these bloody angina pectoris attacks and generally a bit dispirited though this and next month are when the very good things should happen (astrologically). I already have intimations that they will.

But you, dear, dear Brenda, do you think I wanted to miss you yesterday at the screening? I had visions of us sitting side by side, my hand in yours in your lap, perhaps brushing your adorable pussy. Strange that I have so many unmentionable visions of you and me in strange positions.

Tomorrow Friday, I have to go to a reception for Mr. Gimpel at the German Consulate, between 6 & 8:00 P.M. Undoubtedly he will be asked to play a number or two. I hate these ceremonies but think this one may be different.

I heard you and Bob and Anne did a wonderful tape on a subject I mentioned to you recently. And you played Lisa! How droll! Did you enjoy it?

And you, dearest Brenda, how is it with you these days? I hope all goes well.

Are you still reading Marie Corelli? I hope you carry on till the very end of the book because it's the latter part which is so wonderful. I won't say why now because I want you to discover it for yourself.

Believe me, I am thinking of you all the time. Why I don't phone beats me. It goes back to my traumatic days on the phone when in the Western Union. (You probably read about this if you read *Tropic of Capricorn*—and if you haven't read that book you must. I can always give you a copy if you need one.) But first finish Corelli. That last part has something in it for you, for me, for all of us. You'll see. Don't gloss over anything. All is relevant and important.

So much for the social, the literary, and the cerebral. You are made of flesh and blood. So am I. Let's get down to your corporeal being. Brenda-in-the-flesh! How are you, dear Brenda? Do you still think of me in a physical way? Do you lust for me? I certainly do for you—and in a very pure way, if this doesn't sound incongruous to you. I mean that when I think of your body and your sex it's just as clear as if I were thinking of the workings of your intricate mind. It sounds crazy, doesn't it? I am not being pious or Puritanical. I love your cunt, your teats, your thighs, your ass, just like any good old lecher. Only I love them all more arduously—I think. On the other hand, what with my recent attacks of angina pectoris, I have an uneasy feeling that if you ever extended me any real favors I might die in your arms. "What better way to die?" you may say. Right! Only I don't want to die just yet. I don't want to leave you. Can't you figure a way in which we could have some measure of enjoyment without the fatal risks? Do you follow me? Am I off my rocker? You know me pretty well now. In fact, I would say "damn well." We meet in our dreams, we rock each other to sleep at night (imaginatively), and God knows what else.

Though I've only known you a short time, I feel I know you intimately. Not your life but you, your emotions, your dreams, your aspirations. And of course every letter I receive from you confirms this suspicion. So much so that when we meet for just a few minutes—kiss and run—I feel content, satisfied, fulfilled. So you see, dear Brenda, I run the whole gamut with you.

If we haven't made love here below we have in dream and reverie. And perhaps those are the best fucks, eh what?

I must leave off now. Day is finished. I am just a bit weary, but horny at the same time—can you beat it? Maybe I was born horny, being a Capricornian with Venus in the natal house and Mars and La Lune in your fucking Scorpio. Nuf said.

I love you! Forgive my silence and seeming neglect.

Ever yours,

HENRY

* * * * * * * * * * * * * * (These are for the imaginary fucks)

•

There were certainly two aspects to our relationship—one fantasy, the other reality. In all the erotic letters and certain passages in other letters, it becomes fantasy. The idea that I did not make love to anyone, because I was not making love to him, was part of the fantasy. Henry's ego was such that he would not accept my going to anyone other than him for anything, including making love.

In reality he knew that I had a boyfriend, but he became so sensitive to being reminded of it that eventually I avoided any mention of my contemporary male friends. When Henry would ask how I managed to suppress my sexual drive, I assured him,

After receiving all those pictures from me Henry reciprocated with one of himself that was taken in Paris in the early thirties.

Henry went over this one with a magnifying glass before deciding we should meet.

Taken by his friend Man Ray, 1946

(Martin)

(Martin)

Henry loved Martin's shots of me and asked if Martin could do a portrait of us. Henry ventured out to the studio for these in 1979. (*Martin*)

For Brenda Happy Birthday 11/10/77   Henry Miller, 1977

"For Brenda Venus. A ray of that wondrous light which illumines as well as glows unceasingly"—Henry Miller, 1979

At Henry's in 1979 (*Douglas Stroke*)

Christmas 1979. Lawrence Durrell was showing me Henry's Paris. Anaïs, Henry and Lawrence were frequently at the Dôme.

"I work out a lot, plus I have ballet, gym, yoga, and running.
He would say, "Hmm, hmm," with a crooked little smile and
that would be the end of that.

•

Same day—Saturday

Beloved—

It's now 10:05 P.M. I thought it was ten to one A.M. Where am I?
Who am I? You've got me completely at your mercy—not just with
your physical charms but with your whole being. I am in 7th Heaven!
Everyone tells me I look great and I reply always—"It's love!" or "It's
Brenda!" I never know where my Brenda may be nor do I wonder very
much—I know wherever she is she is with me, body and soul. No,
Brenda, we are like Siamese twins—you can only cut us apart.

Some time soon I must see your house again! Especially since it's
been denuded—all except for my water colors and yours!

Had letter from Irving Stettner tonight. Saw *People* and our photo.
Thought you looked *magnifique!*

You know, I lost my dear friend and brother-in-law Lilik Schatz of
Jerusalem the other day. Seems like "they" are dying like flies around
me. And what keeps me alive and throbbing? Brenda Venus, one time
resident of Hattiesburg and Biloxi. Biloxi—there's where I take imaginary strolls with you—beneath those live oak trees planted by some
Greek. I always see you alone, never with your mother or a nun, God
save the mark.

Reminds me of the time I took over my father's business (for a year
or so)—he was too ill to go to work. The first time I open the safe I find
a drawer full of dirty postcards and condoms bathing in talcum powder!!
So he's human! I said to myself. But it's always a bit of a shock to know
your parents did the same thing (once upon a time) as you, *n'est-ce pas?*

Paper is running out and time, too. They're calling me for dinner.
Up with the Nobel Prize!

Selah! All yours!

HENRY

P.S. You, me, and Mississippi!! Always a blue-violet dream. We fit
together—and no talcum powder needed. HM

LOVE!!!!

I will leave you now looking *magnifique* and feeling the same, I trust. I hold you tight to me, so that I feel your entire imprint on me. It's delicious. Your inamorata, Henry.

Could write more but my eyes give out!

Were you thinking strongly of me today?

•

I was. He had not received the Nobel Prize. Everyone who knew and loved him understood he needed to be alone. He was so heartbroken that he phoned Lawrence Durrell to discuss the matter, and Durrell told him that he had personally met one of the chief men and asked him point-blank. The reply was "Monsieur Durrell, I think I must tell you that we are waiting for him to become respectable."

Henry's reply to that was "Never in my life will I become respectable. I'll never be anything else. I don't think I can ever stop writing. I might write crap after a while, but I'll still be writing what I feel. I may die with a pen in my hand."

I think the anger finally got him out of bed.

A long time later, when Henry was in a story-telling mood, he explained what he felt had happened.

•

I got acquainted with a Swede who was translator from French into English and Swedish and Norwegian. Fine translator, translated Rimbaud, the surrealists, symbolists, and the great French poets very well and I began a correspondence with this man. And then one day he says, "I am going to be in Paris on a certain date, could I see you? I'd like to have a talk with you." And I thought, "nothing better," but to make sure, instead of telling him to come, I make a date in a café on the Blvd. St.-Michel—a broad street leading to the Pantheon. This is a very celebrated spot. I go to meet him there and believe me, within seven minutes of talking to him, I was so fed up with his trivia, his nonsense, that I suddenly said, "Excuse me, oh excuse me—I just thought of it. I have a rendezvous right up the street and I forgot all about it. Will you excuse me?" And I ran away from him. I ran, I just didn't walk. And at the corner where I was supposed to have my rendezvous I turned and I ran and I began zig-zagging through the street in case he followed me.

Now that man happened to be, later on, the head of the literary committee for the Nobel Prize! If he remembered that incident, he must have had it in for me for years.

Same day or night

Dearest Brenda—

You forgot the book on Writing you asked for.

Now about Writing. Letters are different from other forms of writing. They are spontaneous, intimate, and from the heart. My book about Writing wouldn't help you. I'm afraid no one can help except your own self. First off you have to learn to read properly (or look at a painting in the right way). As you do this you will remember certain things about style which you overlooked before. Art is an everyday thing. It's a way of looking at life, people, circumstances. You see what others see but more. You see what you put into it yourself.

I won't go on with this now—I'm getting chilly. Here is another very wonderful author for you to get acquainted with—R. H. Blyth, an Englishman, a Zen man. Wonderful!

I must leave you now. So good of you to come. You're an angel.

Love,

HENRY

Friday P.M.

Dear dear Brenda—

I got a letter from you today (unexpectedly). Hurrah! Don't know if I'll have the time or energy to respond to everything.

First: *Ecstasy.* I saw it in Paris in the early 30's and wrote a chapter on it—called *Extase* in *français.* Remember praising it because the rhythm was so deliberately slow. Yes, the woman in it whom you mention was a wonderful physical specimen and not above revealing her charms. I didn't know she was a Scorpio. If I remember rightly, the book my chapter was in was called *The Cosmological Eye* (published by New Directions, N.Y.). Either in that book or another I had a whole chapter on my (then) favorite films and favorite actors and actresses.

Did I tell you I had a visit the other day from a Danish female writer (32), quite beautiful and attractive who gave me her book *Deliver Us from Love*. I'll lend you it after two or three people have read it. You'll enjoy it, I'm sure. She's very frank, candid, forthright, sharp as a whip with a sense of humor. (Another Scorpio.) I could have fallen in love with her (if not for you).

But what I started to tell you about is that this A.M. on going to the bathroom (a little too late, alas!) I fell back on the toilet seat with a terrific bang (slipped), hurt my back and put another gash in my arm. Besides, I was severely shaken up—it lasted all day. Otherwise, I would have phoned you—but that slip took the starch out of me. Following it I had 3 or 4 attacks of angina pectoris. This is a lousy ailment which gives you real anguish. You know you're not going to die but you feel terrible anguish and constriction in arms and chest.

So—you wrote a treatment for a love story. Great! Do you think Clint can play an ardent lover? I wish I could write you just one screenplay—but either I lack the talent or the challenge doesn't interest me. I can only go on telling the story of my life, it seems. And to that there is no end.

Brenda, it's strange how I get side-tracked in writing you. I sit down intending to talk about you, your body, your temperament, your ripeness for love and I end up writing about everything else under the sun. (I could lick you all over and especially that little crevice between the legs. I imagine I could fuck you morning, noon, and night, but common sense tells me that's out of the question. But nobody can stop me from fucking your head off—in my imagination. One of the tragedies of old age is that one can be very horny, yet not have an erection. But I imagine something similar happens to women at any age, *non?*)

Let me wind up on this note—that your gorgeous body is an eternal temptation.

I ache all over from my fall in the bathroom. So I will stop and say good night to you, dear Brenda, in all your adorable parts.

More soon! Yes, we will get together here, there, or elsewhere soon.

HENRY

Monday

Darling Brenda—

The sight of you and the feel of you is still with me. It's you, you, that gets me, throws me for a loop, etc., etc., etc. It's as if I saw you for the first time—last night. Out of this world. Brimming over with love, sex, adoration, compassion, *tout, tout.*

I want to go into the next room and paint but am glued here as my doctor has only the phone number in this room.

My dear, darling Brenda, what I really ache to do is to gently crush your pussy *(le petit chat)* through your dress or naked flesh, whichever, however. It is almost an obsession with me. But it's like holding a condensed version of you, you in the form of a flower—pansy, gladiola, orchid or whatever; we are always so close to this state. I'm sure you are aware of it. But it's as if there were a secret pact between us—thus far and no farther! Yet, when you throw your arms around me it's with body and soul. You give all of yourself—and a little, or a great deal, more. It seems sacrilegious therefore to talk about the missing flower, does it not? But I would not be H.M. if I didn't. In fact, it's very unlike H.M. to talk about it. He usually acts first and thinks afterwards.

Do I bore you with this male prattle? I hope not. And I hope it does not diminish me in your eyes. Do you like this paper? Seems warmer, more passionate, *n'est-ce pas?* Maybe I am having my menstrual period. Men have them too, you know, only when they do, they bleed from all the pores in their body, and the brain included.

And then it seems as if the heavens contained only the most delicate weight *(les poids délicats du ciel).* And you, my beloved, are floating there in the clouds, weightless and wingless.

(Whatever made Terence Young think of my bathroom, entering yours?)

Yes, you are a beauty—a classic beauty—*du temps ancien.* Sicilian to the eye and hand, Spanish in haughtiness, stoic in Indian fashion—and universal, like Mother Earth itself in your ability to love. You are the lover who plays on muted strings, to paraphrase my idol Knut Hamsun.

Do continue deeper into Maggi Lidchi's book, there is much in it just for you—and coming from a real woman. You will see.

I wondered whatever put it into your head last night to say, "We could argue greatly." Why would we ever argue? I blush just to offer a passing criticism—of my goddess. And you, I sense that you accept me wholly—no ifs or buts or maybes. *Alors, à quoi bon de se discuter? Je t'aime profondément, je suis à toi seule.*

HENRY

P.S. Still no letter from you? And you, did you receive mine yet? It would be a pity if it were lost for I blessed you in a thousand different ways. And herein are a few more!

H.M.

10/13/76

Good morning, my lovely Brenda. How are you today?

I had two strange experiences today. It's my day to visit my heart doctor for a checkup. (Charles couldn't take me so Tony did.) On the way in he put on a cassette of Chopin's works—very good. When we got to the doctor's place we found the elevator out of order. I couldn't climb the 2 flights of stairs to his office so Tony carried me up in his arms as if I were a child.

On the way home he put a cassette on of his favorite piece of music—Beethoven's famous 9th Symphony. For all the music I have listened to in my life, I must confess I had never listened to this fabulous work. When it was through I said to myself, "One has to be somewhat mad to compose such a glorious Ode to Joy."

I tell you this because I feel so strongly that for the great creations a bit of madness is absolutely necessary. Shakespeare was touched, so was Rabelais. Of course for cinema and T.V. scripts normality is the order of the day.

The letters I receive from madmen I save. The others go to the library. Yours are kept in a trunk to be opened after my death.

Keep writing me, dear Brenda, even if the letters must be spaced out. You give me warmth, encouragement, and inspiration.

I sometimes wonder if my letters get too personal, too vulgar, too intimate. Do they? You always proclaim that you love them. I hope it's true because you are going to receive many more, if I live long enough.

I must soon stop as the little piece of missing flesh in my rear end makes sitting an ordeal.

I like the way you close your letters. Always something new. You are not only a darling of the gods, you are a gem—a Kohinoor.

See you Thursday—not before, I am afraid. I must have fallen sound asleep last night—never heard you or felt your kiss.

So long now,

HENRY

Sunday 10/23/76

Darling Brenda,

Just a few words now—more tomorrow—to tell you how very precious you are to me. When I saw your letter on my desk yesterday my heart fell. I had so looked forward to seeing you again. However I thoroughly understand.

I woke up feeling empty—missed you so much *and* thinking that the great event I am looking for (promised by the astrologers)—this great event has already happened. *It's you!* How blind of me not to recognize it!

That letter you read to me yesterday was the greatest tribute any woman ever paid me—do I really deserve it? You always speak only of my virtues, never my faults. That's such a wonderful thing. (Val is just the contrary—yet you are both Scorpios!)

So I will see you soon. How very very wonderful. Like the answer to a prayer.

Bless you, bless you, my darling Brenda!

HENRY

Same day—10:00 P.M.

Darling Brenda!

Just reread that marvelous letter. You know, my dear, you express yourself unbelievably well in letters. Probably because it's a medium for which one needs *heart*. And you are all heart, from head to toe. Yes, I may have *The Heart of a Boy* next time you come. I am looking forward to receiving two more copies. It's *Cuore* in Italian—just "Heart" which is so much more accurate. I expect you to *love* this little book. I also got two more old favorites—one by Pierre Loti (in English) called *Disenchanted*, about a love affair with a woman in a Turkish harem. And *On Overgrown Paths* by Knut Hamsun, written from the Insane Asylum and the Old People's Home, where he was incarcerated for being a traitor, like Ezra Pound. Both touching and romantic. Reading very slowly. Tonight Sava was explaining the possible meaning of one of Cendrars' early works—*Moravagine*. "Death to the Vagina." Droll, what?

Hey! I made another water color this afternoon. A real goofy one, but I think quite interesting. I had given it up as hopeless, went in for a short nap, back to the work table and made something come through by sheer force of will. Don't need to be ashamed of it. I spelled out in the body of some unknown animal the word sarasota—meaning a town in Florida. Why? No reason. Best reason of all is always "no reason." Did mother think when cohabiting with father what "it" would look like out of the womb? I reckon not.

"Away down South in Dixie . . ." It's coming back to me. You are my dixieland sweetheart, my Pensacola flapper. My picayune Graziella . . ." Away, away . . ."

I lost my heart in Dixie, and man I don't ever want it back again. It's all yours. Live on, O my Muse, my Inamorata. *Live on!!!*

HENRY

SCENARIO

Early Days

Rereading a book I read long, long ago *(Heart of a Boy)*, I was impressed by certain resemblances between the life of Italian boys and the ones I knew in dear old Brooklyn. For one thing we both understood what Carlyle referred to in one of his books, *Heroes and Hero Worshippers*. We admired the boys who inspired our admiration unashamedly. We also were hard on weaklings and dummies. Now and then we acknowledged that so-and-so was a real saint. He was apt to be six or eight years older than us, poor, hauling coal and wood for a living (this early in life), but with a golden heart. Johnny Paul, an Italian teenager, was in my humble opinion a saint; though I wasn't yet quite aware of what saints were supposed to be like. (I was brought up in a Presbyterian Church, not a Catholic one. We didn't talk of Saints and Virgin Mary's there.)

We tried to win the favor of our heroes. Were they to give us a smile or a pat on the back we were in Seventh Heaven.

In my particular neighborhood we kids never used the word "prostitute," nor did we ever hear of it. Whore was our word. And one of our little girl friends was known as the whore of the neighborhood. Jenny was her name and she was a charming, gentle creature who may have shaped my image of "whore" very early in life. When I first got to Paris I made friends with the whores very readily, one of the first short stories I wrote there was about "Mlle. Claude." Somehow they were always aware that I regarded them differently than most men.

To get back to Jenny. We used to pretend to fuck her in someone's cellar—"a penny a crack." Actually, all we did was to touch genitals. But we got almost as great a thrill from doing that as we did out of "a good fuck" later on.

The word I always use about my early days (from five to ten) is *golden*. In my memory this period stands out (even today) above all the others. Perhaps because everything was "new" to me. And I was a fast learner. Not only did I learn in the streets but at home, seated at one end of my grandfather's bench. (He was a coat maker and worked for my father, who was a Fifth Avenue tailor.) I would sit at his bench reading one of my many books, sometimes I read to him aloud. Sometimes he handed me a couple of pieces of cloth, a needle and thread, and told me to make something to please my father when he would come home. (Even at that early date there was a conspiracy afoot to make me a tailor, too.)

Sometimes I brought Stanley (my first friend) to the room my grandfather worked in. We would play with my toys while my grandfather sang "Shoofly, don't bother me"—his favorite ditty.

In that same room, on a rainy day, I recall singing songs in a hearty, lusty voice. And my aunt, working in the kitchen nearby, would come out and clap her hands, kiss me, beg me to sing some more.

Years later, many years later, with Val or Tony on my back, I would trudge through the forest teaching them songs like "Yankee Doodle Dandy" and the like. They loved these jaunts through the forest.

One of the outstanding things about this period, which is so vivid in my memory, is that already we were incipient psychologists. We (Stanley and I) had every boy in the neighborhood sized up. The heroes like Eddie Carney and Lester Reardon, stood apart. When Lester Reardon walked down North First Street—just one block—I stood in awe, watching him. If he had been the Pope I could not have paid more reverence. Then there were the potential criminals like Alfie Letcha and Johnny Goeller. As a matter of fact, they both ended up in Sing Sing.

Sing Sing! A notorious prison on the Hudson. One day, again many years later, the ex-warden of Sing Sing comes to visit me at my office in the Western Union Telegraph Co., where I was then employment manager. He came, representing some Catholic organization which tried to rehabilitate ex-convicts. I told him immediately that I was forbidden to hire ex-convicts. He disregarded my remark and began telling me he would pay with his life for any misdemeanor on the part of anyone he sent me. I was so taken by his earnestness that I hired three or four ex-convicts the next day. Not only did I find them efficient and reliable (which the young boys were not!) but, on leaving the service, they would always come to thank me for what I had done and leave me some token gift, such as a ring or a watch. Often they blessed me. . . .

Wednesday

Brenda—

Darling, you looked ravishing yesterday in your ballet costume. (Wish we could go to dinner in that rig.)

I have been wanting to write you ever since you left yesterday—and here it is noon *next day*! So damn many chores and unexpected visitors.

Wanted to tell you that from time you left me until 8:00 A.M. today no chest pain—but at 8:00 A.M. violent pains in the arm. Now diminishing. An old doctor friend of mine (from Bermuda) will be visiting me in a few minutes. My guess is *not* gas but *psychosomatic*. You are the cause and the cure—*both*. Don't you agree?

Anyway I feel great. Must stop—doctor just came.

Love

HENRY

TO BRENDA LA BIEN AIMÉE!

After many moons of silence
Comes a little song again
For my beloved Brenda
Of earth, stars and sea
And other places with good places not to mention
Although filled with good intention
Such as the ever fascinating place
Between the limbs, the bosom curved
Like the hull of an ocean liner
The strong feminine feet and thighs
From on high and enlacing near
And perhaps embracing
All too strenuously, like life itself
And all her loved ones, mortal
And immortal, with flesh, soul,
Spirit, gray matter and all the
Convolutions of the perfumed flesh
That ever reside enticingly beneath the silkiest raiment worn
Only by queens, ballerinas and
Goddesses of terrestrial origins
Product of physical and divine

Love that knew no bounds
Forever in heat and lust and
Cradled in spiritual zest
So be it with Brenda, cherubim and seraphim, ethereal,
Corporeal, magnetic commune
The Polar Star, always pointing heavenward whilst inspired
By the unholiest dreams of Man, woman, god or devil.

HENRI

1977

Blessed Brenda—

There is still a pile of unanswered mail facing me but I felt I could afford to take a break and say a few words about your Jelinda, the deep South (magnolias, Spanish moss, etc.) and "education."

Your friend Jelinda DeVorzon is all you told me to look for, and more. She has inner beauty as well as outer, is delicate, most considerate *and* what you people (Southerners) call a "real lady."

She wanted to know the title of that Dostoievsky book—it came to me in my sleep last night—*Crime and Punishment.* Jelinda seemed to stress the need for more education. In my opinion that is not only wrong but unnecessary. What we need is not more knowledge but wisdom. I mean wisdom of life. How to survive and make the most of it on this fucking (fucked up) planet. Made so, I feel, not by any Creator, but by man himself. But by more wisdom I don't mean Hindu gurus, lamas, teachers, etc. One may find it in a very ordinary person. The "ignorant" often have more real wisdom than the educated ones.

Soon as you give me Jelinda's address we'll get busy and write a few publishers or/and booksellers to send her some of the books I have "enjoyed." Maybe they did my soul good. I think you have read most of them—viz: *Boyhood with Gurdjieff* by Fritz Peters; my two Vols. of *Book of Friends; Earth Man* by Maggi Lidchi; *Look and Move On* by Mohammed Mrabet, and so on. I don't think we should read for instruction but to give our souls a chance to luxuriate. Feelings come before intellect. (But you gals know all about that!)

What is it about the "Southern belle" that makes men fall at their feet? I think more than the ability to surrender. (I know, of course, it is only a "seeming" surrender, but it is what enchants and undermines men, deflates their egos, brings out the chevalier and the troubador in them.

Your friend seems to be more at peace with herself than you, if I may say so. She has succeeded in her career—whatever that is. Sometimes I think, my dear Brenda, that you fight too hard, struggle too much. You ought to let chance or Fate play more of a part in your life!

I hope this last doesn't offend. You know your troubles will really begin when you get to the top! Adoration is only for the gods, ordinary mortals (that includes "stars") only get mansions, Rolls Royces, and headaches.

To look at it from another angle . . . If all's wrong with the world and if the Creator allowed things to be as they are, what then can poor mortals do? They can't correct *"cosmic mistakes."*

Well, my back aches from so damn much writing and reading today. I'm going to quit and take a lie down. Maybe I'll talk to you before dinner.

I love every bone in your body, every muscle, every blood vessel— but most of all *you yourself!*

Still more love.

Your abject one, meaning completely devoted one.

Henry

P.S. Sent photo of you alone to my *German* biographer. He wanted to know what "inamorata" means. (Beloved)

Same day—Tuesday

My dear, noble Brenda—

You seemed to be in a rather sombre mood today. Also ultra-sensitive. Before I go much further, I must remind you that birth and death are the two indisputable facts of life, one must look them squarely in the face. It does not become you—it is not seemly, as they say—for you to suddenly weep, even a little, at the mention of certain unpleasant things. I have always maintained that if Life is good then so must Death be. They are both mysteries, not disasters.

And this leads me somehow to mention once again the *Lamed* Vov. You may have noticed that Jesus had 12 disciples—and they were real nobodies. King Arthur had 12 Knights of the Round Table and his great favorite seduced Arthur's wife Guinevere. There are 12 signs of the Zodiac—and it is hard to say which is better than another. All these twelves are components of 36 or *Lamed* Vov.

This brings me to Martin, the business manager. Though I found him a most intelligent critter I also am a bit leery of his "knowledge."

He is so Jewish, in that time-ordained way of the Jews. You must stick to your guns, to your own anarchic nature, your quixotic, rebellious nature, your instinctiveness, and your unfailing intuition. Martin is by nature a Teacher. He wants to impose his ideas on others. All of which simply means—"Beware!"

Often we conquer not by storming the castle but by ruse, subterfuge, trickery, and other shenanigans. And then too we must acknowledge our own helplessness. All of us need help, even the greatest. And here is where love comes in, Love, not Mind, not Reason, not Intellect—Love combined with Chance. For Chance too plays its role in our lives. And chance is more apt to befall the calm, certain one than the anxious one. Anxiety is a curse, like ambition. One must be neither too cocky nor too humble. Just "ready"—for whatever. Remember, *It* decides, not you, not me, not President Carter.

I got out of bed shortly after you left and put in a good stint. Still no writing nor painting, but doing what had to be done. I feel good. I hope this missive doesn't sound preachy. I'm just blowing off steam. And don't think that you or I are *Lamed Vovniks*. We are too self-interested, too egocentric. We are just raw material. Please don't weep any more. And don't worry about it affecting your looks. You will always be beautiful and alluring, in fair weather or foul.

I have been wondering if you managed to get the air-conditioning yet. Had a funny, abrasive thought about it. You may remember that good old Benjamin Franklin advocated (even back then) going about naked. In the confines of one's home, *naturellement*. After I left your home that night, I seemed to remember the position of a tall mirror—probably in your bedroom. And I wondered if you had the luxurious habit of going around stark naked, perhaps coming to a halt now and then before that mirror, and while admiring yourself, caressing your teats and your discreet little pussy. I could imagine it vividly. I'm sure you have done it frequently. And ditto in the hot tub. How can you not? The temptation is irresistible. As Oscar Wilde said once, "If there are temptations one can overcome then they are *not* temptations."

Enuf. I take it that when you asked for reading matter you must have abandoned Loti's *Disenchanted*. I hope not. I hope you merely put it aside for a while.

Look at chapter on Anaïs in *Colossus* first. See again analogies and resemblances between you, Corelli and herself. And, when you have nothing better to do, read this letter *backwards*. I love you dearly. I will embrace you Thursday.

HENRY

•

It started to rain as we were driving down Sunset Boulevard one night on our way to the Imperial Gardens for dinner. Even though we had been looking forward to our evening out for quite a while, storing up topics to discuss over sashimi and hot saké, I asked Henry if he wanted to turn back. I hated driving in the rain, and Henry had a great fear of getting chilled and developing pneumonia. But Henry said he was "ravenous" and there really wasn't anything to eat at his house. So we continued. All the way he kept telling me to slow down on the curves. Finally I was going under twenty-five miles an hour and the Porsche was complaining.

The restaurant sits on a steep hill overlooking Hollywood. The best parking I could find was near the rear entrance, but on quite a hill. Henry took one look at the puddles we'd have to wade through and told me he just couldn't do it. All he had to walk in were his fuzzy white slippers. I told him to stay in the car, and went in to find the owner, Lyle, who'd be able to carry Henry in.

A few minutes later I was back in the car. "Henry, Lyle's not here. I'll carry you, okay?"

Henry was nervous, but somehow trusting. "If you think you can do it . . ."

I went around to his door. As he put his arms out to me, I suddenly had a flash of the next day's headlines: HENRY MILLER DROPPED BY ACTRESS!! This did wonders for my adrenaline. I scooped up Henry and set off across the broken parking lot. And that's when I remembered I was wearing high heels! It was too late to turn back. With each step I felt for cracks in the pavement.

Halfway there, one of Henry's legs slipped off my arm. Henry asked me if I was okay. I said, "Sure, just think about your weight lifting and keep a tight grip around my neck." Henry began to feel to me as if he weighed a ton. He was holding on to me so tightly I was almost choking, but I had to go on. I got my arm back around his other leg. I kept walking. The door was closer. Someone opened it, and we were safe!

The rest of the evening was laced with laughter and lots of saké. Henry regaled me with tales of his hero Blaise Cendrars' death-defying exploits—such as driving across the Sahara with one arm freshly chopped off! I don't think either of us ever enjoyed one evening out as much as the one we had that night.

•

2/26/77

Dear, dear Brenda—

What a woman you are! Come all the way here to drop letters in my mail box but don't make any effort to see me (or did you?). Yes, there is some resemblance between you and the Filipovna woman—only she is thoroughly something else. You know, I do believe the Russians are enigmatic, perhaps because they are of Asia where everything is mysterious. People say that the Russian tongue is a very wonderful one—certainly the décor of physical background—the steppes, for one thing—very marked, very powerful influence, colors all they do.

I have always been interested and intrigued by women who fall in love with men much older than themselves. I notice, for one thing, that they are usually very interesting conversationalists, lead risky (not risqué) lives, etc., etc. But Dostoievsky's Nastasya is an extraordinary female, whether Russian or Chinese or Arabian. Unique. In a way so was my ex-wife, Mona of the Tropics. (She had Gypsy, Roumanian, and Jewish blood. Her blood counted heavily. Gave a tone to all her actions.) Of course she was also an actress—both on and off stage. And somehow the actress in a woman always gets me. (I suppose I like multiple personalities.) And I usually like a touch of evil (whether in man or woman). The other night, at dinner table, Tony was remarking that there were a goodly number of women in my life with whom sex was not necessary. Nearly all these women, I recollect now, were highly interesting talkers and characters.

Why am I telling you all this? First off, sorry to say, to get my mind off the pain in my foot—rather bad tonight tho' it continues to improve in looks. Strange, I have ailments of one sort or another, but my general health is good. Every day now I feel a little stronger, but when it comes to walking, I am a mess still. And I feel humiliated hanging like a cripple on the arm of a beautiful woman—especially in a large restaurant, where all eyes are on us. How *are* your beautiful eyes now? Don't

henry miller 444 **ocampo** drive -- **pacific palisades** california 90272

Dear, dear Brenda —   2/26/77

What a woman you are! Come all the way here to drop letters in my mail box but don't make any effort to see me. (or did you?)

Yes, there is some resemblance between you and the Filipina woman — only she is thoroly Russian and you are thoroly something else. You know, I do believe the Russians are enigmatic, perhaps because they are of Asia where everything is mysterious. People say that the Russian tongue is a very wonderful one — certainly the décor or physical background — the steppes, for one thing — very marked, very powerful influence, colors all they do.

I have always been interested and intrigued by women who fall in love with men much older than themselves. I notice, for one thing, that they are usually very interesting conversationalists, lead risky (not risqué) lives, etc. etc.

P.S. I could write loads more. And I will. Beg with me! I have infinite patience and at the same time I am one of the most impatient of men. Do you really seem like the orphan in Brooklyn?

But Nadasya (not "Natasha") is an extraordinary female, whether Russian or Chinese or Arabian. Unique. In a way so was my ex-wife Mona of the Tropics. (She had Gypsy, Roumanian and Jewish blood. Her blood counted heavily. I ave a love to all her actions.) Of course she was also an actress — both on and off stage. And somehow the actress in a woman always gets me. (I suppose I like multiple personalities.) And I usually like a touch of evil (whether in man or woman). The other night, at dinner table, Twinka was remarking that there were a goodly number of women in my life with whom sex was not necessary. Nearly all these women, I recollect now, were highly interesting talkers and characters.

Why am I telling you all this? First off, sorry to say, to get my mind off the pain in my foot — rather bad tonight tho' it continues to improve in looks. Strange, I have ailments of one sort or another, but my general health is good. Every day now I feel a little stronger, but when it comes to walking I am a mess still. And I feel humiliated hanging read over prolonged periods. A bit at a time. I'll stop now with a very warm squeeze. You're such a contradiction—angel with sex.

HENRY

P.S. I could write loads more. And I will. Bear with me! I have infinite patience and at the same time I am one of the most impatient of men. Do I really seem like Orpheus in Brooklyn?

3/12/77

Dear Brenda—

I seem to be in the doldrums. How are you? It's going to rain, I believe—I can feel it in my bones. Well, I finished my chapter on Joe Gray—it was very simple. (Maybe I told you this in my last.)

Today I had a card from the Gotham Book Mart, saying they sent you *The Joy of Man's Desiring* by Jean Giono. They told me which books I asked for were on hand and so I ordered the following for you:

1. *The Collected Plays of Synge* (in which you will find *Playboy of Western World*)
2. *Victoria* by Knut Hamsun
3. *Dead Souls* by Gogol.

So, you will have something to feed on when time hangs heavy on your hands.

I received a letter from Anaïs' husband, Rupert Pole, saying he wanted to see me—to tell me good things. I wrote him to come this afternoon or Sunday afternoon—couldn't reach him on the phone. I wonder what he has to tell me.

And then Lisa called saying she thought she could get a grant to do a documentary about me. I told her I wasn't too keen about it but would do it to please her.

And then I received a magazine *(The Lost Generation)* devoted almost entirely to me but the editor and his assistant (a woman) play hell with me. I "have never written anything memorable," he writes. She writes a persnickety column about me, largely unfavorable. One wonders why they bothered to put out this issue.

So it goes. Oof! What a chatterbox I am! Excuse me, but I know you like to hear the news.

HENRY

3/25/77

Dear, dear Brenda—

What a pleasure to talk to you earlier today! I had just put a stack of mail on my desk—a terrible slew of it this time. Then I found yours and recovered my senses. Now I have answered those I deemed necessary to answer and the rest are in the waste basket. I needed to receive your letter—I was beginning to think you had given me the go by.

I always have so much to tell you but only give you part of it in my letters. And lately, I fear, I've become garrulous.

I love you more and more all the time. You're so strong, so stable, so sure of yourself! Today you gave me the greatest compliment a man could hope for. If I am that "real man," you certainly are that "real woman."

(By the way, that peeing in a cup is fantastic. But why not? Only isn't a cup rather small for what your bladder holds?)

Without having become intimate with you, I somehow "divine" your body. In my half sleep I go over it bit by bit, always coming to rest at the mound of Venus (or should I say "the Cavern" of Venus for I have even strayed in there—and got lost, of course, not because of its unusual size but because of its labyrinthine splendors). Do I make myself clear? I said "I" get lost, not my prick. That has not the right of entry as yet. And if it never does it won't really matter. It's the *woman* who interests me. I won't say her cunt doesn't—only it's secondary. Seeing your face, your luminous eyes, a bit of bare flesh—(teats or thighs) does for the nonce. As I said, I believe you are really chaste, despite all the sexual paraphernalia you wrap yourself in. Anyway, chaste or lascivious, I love you to the bone. I always get an erection when you leave—delayed reaction. Be good to yourself. Soon we'll make it again to the Imperial Gardens.

P.S. I could write more but my eye is giving out. *Je t'embrasse tendrement.*

HM

4/23/77
Same day—little later

Darling Brenda—

You looked *wonderful* today—radiant, sexy, erotic, sensual. And I want you to know immediately that I took a great liking to your brother. He's quite a man, I should say. And his accent is enchanting. I enjoyed every moment of our conversation. (Now I can imagine what Joe your father was like!)

Once again I forgot to put in your hands the Omarr book. Monday will be mailing you the new Capra Press book—*Four Visions of America*. I like only my own. See for yourself!

I must stop now. My sight is giving out. Too much reading.

Your loving three year old!

HENRY

•

At this time I was away much of the time, either giving fashion shows for the family store in Mississippi, or acting in a film on location. I wrote Henry regularly, but from the more distant locations, the delays in the mails could be long. If two or three days passed without word from me, he would begin to worry.

•

8:45 P.M. Sat. 5/17/77

Dear Brenda—

How wonderful to hear your voice again! I feel as if you have been away a long time. Lying in bed a while ago, I tried to picture us at the Imperial Gardens, but by us I meant you, Lisa Lu, Hoki, and myself. I don't think I could pull it off. When it comes to telling a woman you no longer love her, I am a great coward. I don't want to hurt her feelings, never realizing that by failing to tell her everything I am causing her more pain and suffering.

Anaïs Nin and I used to talk of this often. Anaïs could lie like a trooper—but always to save the other person's feelings, never to hurt or inflict punishment.

Americans, more than any other people I can think of, place great emphasis on telling the truth, the whole truth, and nothing but the truth. Older peoples are not so scrupulous or fastidious. For the truth, as well as the lie, can hurt terribly. I guess the truth is that one has to be intuitive, know when to talk and when to shut up, eh?

I can't deny that it gave me a bit of a thrill, or shall I say "corroboration," when Hoki's girl friend told me how often and how beautifully Hoki spoke of me. It's true that I was "an easy mark." On the other hand, it's very difficult for me to say no to a demand. Because, no doubt, I have been a beggar for the greater part of my life. I have heard no, together with a thousand different excuses, so often that it's like the sound of a funeral march in my ears. Always the people who refused me were what is called "respectable" people. (The worst kind!)

And then there were the humorless people! (Like Jesus and Confucius). God save me from them! I can tolerate a scoundrel if he has a good sense of humor.

Why all this, I wonder. Something must have touched me off without my being aware of it. Maybe the reverent way Hoki examined that gift you made me.

Today I received a complimentary copy of *The Book of Lists*. Rather fascinating—not boring as I had imagined it would be. In it was my list of the ten greatest authors, with a photo of Marie Corelli, believe it or not. My tenth author was Isaac Bashevis Singer!

I am slowly ploughing through the book on Jean Giono. In it he mentions a number of times "Que ma joie démure!" Someday soon I hope to lay hands on *The Song of the World* for you. A cosmic treat, in my opinion. I don't know if you noticed, but most of Giono's characters are peasant men and women—rather complete individuals. Giono himself had little to do with the social world. I still adore him! Enuf for tonight. Next week we meet in the flesh. Hallelujah!

Your devoted amour.

HENRI

•

Henry was intrigued by sex, and had accumulated vast anecdotal information on the subject. He thought sex was one of the highest forms of spirituality and art that ever existed. He wanted to educate me in the great sexual philosophies of the

world—he gave me Japanese exotic cards, and books of Tantra
yoga positions which he claimed were the supreme sexual
union of two human beings. He found a book for me on erotic
spirituality, *The Vision of Konarak*. Konarak is one of the largest
temples in India, famous for its erotic sculpture.

I was never able to reconcile fully the two sides of Henry I
knew—the shy, simple, gentle man who gave me subtle lessons
in the beauty of lovemaking through books, art and poetry, and
the other Henry who took such pride in the directness, no
matter how coarse, of so much of his writing about sex.

•

Saturday—near midnight

Darling, beloved—

Impossible to sleep, despite pills, many ups & downs. Can't get you
out of my mind.

Had a wonderful interview today with Kazuko, Anaïs' Japanese
friend. It went hand in glove—like water falling off a duck's back . . .

In the mail this day I received a book on Eroticism in Japan—full of
photos in every lewd, obscene position. They were all from original
works done by Japanese centuries ago, during their "age of innocence,"
when they knew neither sin *nor* guilt. The ironic thing is that today
censorship of everything even hinting of sex is stronger than in any
other country in the world. This is *our* contribution to Japanese culture.

In the course of the interview we rehashed the man-woman relationship as it exists today in Japan. Seems Japan still has a matriarchal
system. Woman allows man to play role of macho, but *she* really rules
the roost. Always gets her way. Yet outwardly servile and obedient. How
clever of her, how wise. Western woman always *fighting* for her rights,
bucking man head on, like two goats.

But listen to this—asking why women show no passion in facial
expression during intercourse, she says, "It would be bad taste." So you
see them in most obscene (and exciting) poses, showing no emotion.
Eyes like slits, mouths like buttonholes. But skin extremely soft and
delicate. And their vulnerable part not the clitoris but the nape of the
neck!

Just had letter from Durrell. Much happier since living all alone.
Has learned to cook and keep house *and* enjoys it. No one to argue with

or yell at. Thinks he has gotten over a life long hurdle—of needing a woman around all the time!

But my darling, here I am rambling again, but what I wanted to let you know is how much I miss you. Am absorbed in thoughts of you all day—all night. By the way, Durrell saw your photo in *People*—thought you were just lovely. Urged me to take good care of you. (Am I doing that, do you still think?) You must get sick and tired of hearing how lovely, how wonderful you are . . .

Oh, yes, letter from Irv Stettner. Found real dictionary giving meaning of Indian tribal names. Here are a few—Biloxi—"first people." Pascagoula—"bread people." Tallahassee—"old friend or old town." Pensacola—"hairy people." Interesting, what! Especially Biloxi. No wonder I love the place and the name. (Where my loved one almost became a nun!)

I finished Preface for book about Gurdjieff and when I see you next I will *lend* you my copy. It is all marked up and I would like to keep it. If you like the book as much as I do, I'll give you a copy of the new edition in January. Then you can mark this copy to suit yourself. I promise you a treat!

And still I haven't told you how I crave you, worship you . . . Everybody tells me I look better and better. And I say, "It's all because of Brenda."

Must stop now. Eye giving out. Guess I'm able now to sleep and dream. I am dreaming more vividly now than ever before in my life. Thanks to you. Only in dreams can I really capture you!

HENRY

Sat. Eve—29th

Dear Brenda—

A little sequel to the geisha theme—according to my friend Veno the geisha is really starved for *love*. Her job is to entertain men, for which she is paid very, very well. In fact, only politicians and rich people can afford to visit a geisha house.

Naturally she is bored with her work, though never showing it. Fed up, and starved for a man's attention and real affection. So she makes love only out of love, though sometimes she accepts handsome gifts from those who can afford them.

How interesting that the very women who are so exciting to men are actually seeking love. (Prostitutes of course are very much like the geisha in this respect. They *work* for the pimp because he shows what she thinks is real love—and he also protects her.)

Today the world seems sex mad, but has forgotten love. Yet love *does* rule the world and those who can have all the sex they want prefer love.

Does this mean that the *actress* demands more personal relationships? Is hungry for *personal* attention? I assume this is so. What think ye, my fair one? From your romantic

HENRY

6:10 P.M. Sunday

Darling Brenda—

For most of this blistering day I lay stretched out on the bed in my pajamas, feeling that it could not possibly be a degree hotter.

I was filled with incongruous thoughts, ranging from highly spiritual to abysmal sexy ones. It started by my recalling a remark of yours at Imperial Gardens one night. Something to the effect that the "cause" of sex was heat—that's why Southerners were great sex artists or sex monomaniacs. Yes, and from that I got to thinking of the hot Asiatic countries, especially India, where sex and religion are strongly allied. And from that to the deception experienced by my deaf friend upon his return to India where he discovered that his Baboji was not the saint he had credited him with being. And I thought of St. Augustine and St. Anthony and others like them, who had been plagued by the flesh but conquered the evils thereof. How mixed up, thoroughly so, is our world. And probably always has been.

I will probably be interrupted in this sequence, but hope to continue after dinner—if heat permits. Sex and love—the perennial problem. No solution either. At least as I view it. If one conquers sex, as did some of the tormented saints, one goes to seed. If one only loves (without sex) one lives in perpetual torment. The imagination never ceases to work, to conjure up devils, panderers, houris, and the most fantastic images. Certainly the imagination is impure, sometimes insane.

(BREAK)

False alarm! No one in kitchen. Guess Viva hasn't come yet.

The spell has been broken. But I will persist, because I really had very interesting thoughts to unfold.

Felt especially "tender" toward you all day. Tender but aware of the flesh. It was as if you had returned from the dead. I had envisioned that, too, in the last 48 hours.

Once, when I answered the phone it was Lisa Lu. Wanted to know how I was. I had never phoned or written her since meeting you. I told her frankly I did not know how to explain my behavior. "It was instantaneous love," I said. To which she replied, "You are so lucky. This doesn't happen very often." She said she was grateful for the time spent with me and would always love me. It ended on a smooth note, with her envying my good fortune.

Yes, me and St. Augustine. Strange alliance for a so-called atheist like me. But I enjoyed, relished, every word out of his mouth. (Hope you get to read the *Stroker* before too long.) It's not easy sledding. Some knotty, gritty passages that make you think and wonder. But what impresses me so much is the need for another *City of God*. For our world is crumbling rapidly. On the toboggan. Going fast. And I like to think that just before it dies there were us two, radiant examples of Love. I don't say pure LOVE. With a capital L and a small e—.

Now I must stop again and look-see. My eyes are smarting.

Think I will continue this tomorrow. . . .

•

We were going to Sydney Omarr's for dinner. As he was introduced to me, Sydney exclaimed, "What a striking resemblance to Anaïs Nin."

Henry said, "Do you think so? I think she looks more like June or Ava [Ava Gardner] than Anaïs, but you're right. There are definite similarities."

We enjoyed an excellent dinner and some champagne. Henry and Sydney talked a lot about old times. I found Sydney perfectly delightful. He made some astrological comments on the reasons why Henry and I were drawn together, but I really didn't understand astrology as Henry did.

As we were going down the elevator after our visit with Sydney,
Henry blurted out, "You know, Sydney is in love with you!" I
told him that was preposterous. We had only just met. But
Henry persisted. "I saw the way he kept looking at you
at dinner."

I think the champagne contributed to the sudden feelings of
jealousy because in reality, Sydney had a beautiful girl friend
with whom he was very much in love. This expression of
jealousy and possessiveness was only the beginning of many
that were to come. I could sense that the stronger his love, the
more jealous he became. Sometimes when he was this way he
was funny and charming, and other times difficult for me
to understand.

•

3/25/77

Darling Brenda—

I repeat—"You were wonderful the other night." I could see that
Omarr took to you immediately—and even Madame Halsey who could
have been a bit catty. You are always radiant, in good form, and with a
full bladder. (Like the Prince of Wales, you never miss an opportunity
to take a leak.)

Today I finished another script for Vol. II. *Book of Friends*—the one
my brother-in-law (Lilik Schatz) of Jerusalem. He comes close to being
the perfect, many-sided man. Like you, he is always self-confident, optimistic, cheerful. A great quality.

I missed what Omarr was telling me about marriage. Was it that I
should try it again or what? I remember you saying, "But he's still mar-
ried!" That seems to stick in your crop. Well, one *can't* say that I didn't
give it a try!

About failing to get "turned on." I must say that the other night you
certainly looked turned on. A funny thing happened next morning—for
a day and a half I had a pain in the wrist. I attribute it to the vigorous
handshake that Bombay Bob gave me.

By the way, don't swallow Sydney's little anecdotes without a grain
of salt. He seems to take pleasure in telling people how I take his girls
away from him. (It's all imaginary.) As for Gloria Swanson, I wouldn't
fuck her with a 10 foot pole, as they say. The other one (in Carmel—

actress Kim Novak) is a horse or mare of another color. Do you know she writes good poetry, is a horse woman and religious—a really serious woman who happens to excite lascivious feelings in men. But I don't think she is at all hypersexed. She's looking for *Love*.

So you fell in love with me all over again! Gosh, that was good to hear and most unexpected. I would have detained you but I knew you had to get up early. You know, you may be sexy (in the head) but you are also chaste in your own way.

Strange that Omarr should have asked me on the phone, "Isn't she a writer?" You may be one, if you aren't one already. Let's say for the nonce that you are an embryonic writer with an erogenous background. How's that?

Well, I will leave you now. I hope all continues to go well and that you will soon know again that "turned on" feeling. Without it life can be pretty dull.

I love you dear Brenda.

9:15 P.M. 5/2/77

Dear Brenda—

Seem filled with energy for some unknown reason—so I spend a little time with you again. You looked more beautiful than ever the other night. You *look* like a star, even if you are not one yet. Maybe that is what gets in your way. Your "starry" looks!

One day I shall kiss you from head to foot. You remember *The Blue Angel* film and that song she sang—"Ich bin von Koff bis Fusz auf Liebe eingesteldt"? We mistranslated it as "Falling in Love Again." Whereas what it means literally is "From head to feet I am imbued with Love." A bit different, eh? And speaking of that film, wasn't Emil Jannings wonderful—and still more wonderful in *The Last Laugh*?

Today I received two volumes of poems from France by I don't know whom. I opened one at random and began reading with great pleasure. The title of this book is *The Poems of A. O. Barnsbooth* by *Valéry Larbaud*. I forgot to say the poems are beautifully translated. Even if you don't care much for poetry, I believe you will love these. I'll show you the book next time. By the way, did the Gotham Book Mart ever send you the two books by that English writer I mentioned? Titles: *I Am Jonathan Scrivner* and *Julian Grant Loses His Way* by Claude Houghton.

Do you act in your sleep or do you make love—or both? Do you want to be another Sarah Bernhardt or a Rachel or an Eleanora Duse—or maybe just your own sweet self? (No answer required.)

My darling Brenda, I think of you all the time and between times, too.

Hold to your faith in yourself—the glory will follow.

All my love!

HENRY

Same day   5/2/77

Dear Brenda—

What I meant to say in my letter earlier today is that laziness (so-called) is just as important as activity. I have a feeling that you believe it is wise or healthy to fill every hour of the day with some (useful) activity. Now that you have enforced leisure, make the most of it! Make your mind empty, if you can. *Play* with your thoughts rather than putting them to some (useful) occupation. It is just as important to empty the mind as it is to fill it. You follow me, don't you?

Your

HENRY

5/3/77

Dearest Brenda—

Last night I wrote you about sleep and laziness. Today I happen to pick up a book by Krishnamurti in which he talks about everything under the sun. I read what he had to say about sleep. But Krishnamurti has one grave fault, I discover—no sense of humor. Also, he talks a lot about love but you wonder if he himself ever was in love with man or woman. Somehow, reading him now, he sounds like a 20th century Confucius. It's all cut and dried. All terribly logical. Also tyrannical in a way. Above all, he is the great "Teacher"—and that's not an enviable role. One should teach without teaching—don't you think? For some strange reason I am presumptuous enough to think that my "balder-dash" has more value than Krishnamurti's preachings.

But, how are you? Are you able to sit up and read this? I keep thinking of you all the time between times, as it were. Did I tell you I took a nice pratfall in the bathroom Monday? Nothing serious except for a good shaking up! You see, the seat in my walker had become detached and when I went to sit down I fell to the floor. My tailbone is still a bit sore. But, for 36 hours I had no pain in my foot. Now it's back again. I think the unexpected fall drove the foot pain away for a while. I had such a sound sleep after the fall—it was glorious.

And *you?* Are you having interesting dreams now? Tonight at dinner Tony was asking me about the Jews and the Chinese. Very much alike in many ways. Probably the oldest and strongest peoples on this earth. (Am I sounding a bit like Krishnamurti?) You are more precious to me every day. Since you are away I get to thinking of your body—inti-mately, I mean. It's so rich, so silky, so beautiful to the touch.

I believe I finished Vol. II of *Book of Friends,* though the publisher may ask me to write a little more. My last chapter about my "best friend the bike" has to do with the anguish of first love. Thank God, you don't cause me anguish. But I'm still shy, aren't I? Must stop now.

> Loads of love from head
> and heart
>
> HENRY

Same Monday Eve   7/18/77

A few hours later . . . Am now in the throes of another sidereal set-up. The astral climate has changed. I am expecting a call from you any minute . . . I hope you understand why I am so patient! That it is not indifference. Nor is it worry. I have had such rude training in waiting—by former loves—that I am almost a veteran at it. The only time I lose control is when you say you are coming at a certain hour and do not show up for two or three hours. Then I am ready to go mad, to get on my knees and pray. Even now, thinking of your long ride to and from work, I get concerned. Anything can happen. I just have to believe in your good fortune, thank your guardian angel.

You know, the older I get, the more intuitive I seem to become. That's why on certain days a heavy cloud may seem to be overhead.

And it usually is, as I learn a few days later. This is the period when my other (better) nature is sharpened, I am often told.

Oh yes, and the other night I awoke from a most wonderful dream. I was in a place similar to Big Sur, only more wonderful still, where the community was like one harmonious being *and* where I could walk, run, drive a car—all my faculties restored. I hated to wake up. It was like a dream of heaven and left me in an ecstatic state for several hours.

Curious too—there was no sex in it. So many of our dreams center around a really good fuck, a fuck in the dark, so to speak. But better than these are what I might call the spiritual ones, where all is and forever was bliss! Don't you agree?

Doesn't it feel good when you know you are thoroughly sexed but you also can do without it—for a time?

Dear Brenda, I often dream of being in bed with you, and it is wonderful beyond words but better still is when you suddenly appear, like an apparition, wearing that da Vinci smile, warm, knowing, chaste. Do you follow me?

I will stop now. I am going to bed in hopes of getting a telephone call from you. We shall meet soon, *n'est-ce pas?*

Your dreamy lover,

HENRY-SAN

●

I told Henry how much I wanted to learn, to read and understand all the important writers and philosophers. He laughed and said that knowing the complete works of great writers and philosophers would not help me be a better person, but if it really meant that much to me, he would be my mentor. I don't think I've ever loved him as much as I did at that moment. It was my dream coming true. I explained to him that in Mississippi, a girl is taught to be a good wife, please her husband, and raise churchgoing children, but it wasn't what I wanted. I had always wanted to choose my own teacher, and the person I had chosen was Henry Miller, of all people, and he had said yes.

We began my education. At first, I would ask innumerable questions and he would send me books on the subjects that interested me. After I had read the book and underlined passages that I didn't grasp, he would explain them to me until I began slowly to understand the writer. If I enjoyed the writer's style, for example, H. Rider Haggard, then Henry would choose one or two more Haggard books for me. Some of these would be hard to find, and when the book finally arrived, after weeks of my waiting for it, Henry would be so excited it was though as if he had found a precious diamond to give to me.

Sometimes over dinner, we would have question-and-answer sessions. As time went on, he gave me works of his favorite writers to sample. I would read bits of poetry to him that I loved, and he in turn would write poetic phrases for me. But books weren't everything. One day Henry showed up in a black limousine and took me to MGM Studios. He had arranged for a private screening of one of our favorite movies— *Anna Karenina* with Greta Garbo.

The two of us sat there alone in the screening room, enveloped in some giant overstuffed chairs, filled with excitement as the credits began to roll. We giggled like two children playing together. But by the end of the film we were both bawling. He pulled out his pressed white handkerchief and dried my eyes. (Henry always had a fresh handkerchief ready for me, as he became accustomed to my sudden tears of joy or sadness.)

The great lesson that I learned from Henry, ultimately, was in allowing me to be part of his life. Observing this frail man, nearly blind, hovering over his ping-pong table, creating a spontaneous and joyous watercolor, then napping like a baby, then getting up and answering his mail for hours on end, shuffling down the hallway in his walker to the bathroom, and back to his desk to write or read and reread old books and new—that was the ultimate mentorship. Henry's life-force, his optimism, creativity, and curiosity, never flagged. He ignored his age and declining health. He loved me and our moments together as if we were contemporaries. He opened my eyes and, as Henry always said, that's as much as anyone can do.

•

More M's for Brenda, plucked from *the skull of a literary gent*—at random.

menstrual

manage

marsupial

maverick

methodology

masticate

Methodist

matriculate

metempsychosis

manipulate

metabolism

mannequin

metronome

murraine

manoeuvre

maul

marine

mule

matutinal

monogamy

mastectomy

masturbation

Names

marijuana

Mohawk

mascot

Monongahela

mandolin

Missoula

mandatory

Missouri

maculate

Manatee

mobility

Massapequa

monotony

Mississippi

mask

Montana

micturate

Mexico

Mogul

Moscow

mendicant

Manitoba

marble

Mauritius

mosque

Marquesas

●

Once, Henry was preparing to go on *The Tonight Show*. He drew up a list of topics he wanted to work into his discussion with Johnny Carson; I was to remind him of these right before he went on.

●

1. Irving and *Stroker—Lamed* Vov.
2. *Disenchanted* and Pierre Loti.

3. *Heart of a Boy!*
4. How I paint without seeing well—one-eyed Jack!
5. What garbage our own publishers put out today.
6. St. Francis waxing (spiritually) strong on *garbage!*
7. Gurdjieff—Book by Fritz Peters.

Do you think I have a chance?? Don't want to talk about *Joey.*

8. The Dalai Lama as opposed to the Pope.
9. Krishnamurti—never on T.V.
10. The coming end of the world—due to "progress."

Am I off my noodle? I know it's virtually impossible—these sub-jects. Most of them taboo.

11. Marie Corelli—The Woman and the Legend. Admired by Lord Gladstone, Lord Tennyson, Oscar Wilde. Sarasate—maestro vi-olinist. A bitch in life!
12. Lou Andreas-Salomé. Why nothing about her from the femi-nists—Women's Lib, etc.?
13. Isaac Singer—Nobel acceptance speech: "Yiddish is a language which contains no word for *weapons*!!" Ignored by newspapers and mags.
14. Cendrars, Knut Hamsun—my favorites. Cendrars dying—an ex-periment.

Am I nuts? *I love you!!!!!*
P.S. Save this in case I need reminders of what to talk about.

NOTES   LETTER TO B.V.   NOTES

No matter whether cunts were large or small, tight or loose.
The carnal side *(charuelle)* Krishna ravaging whole village at any hour of day or night. Women swooning into delight. *Ravage*-fuck. Fucked everything with a cunt—any age, child, bride, mother, grand-mother!
Nonavati (nonentity) invoking Krishna's name whenever he betrayed his wife. "K——wants us to fuck. . . ."
"Please to make dinner now, Endrée, it's getting late." Please to clean stool next time. Please to make beds. Please to take garbage down-stairs. A slave to this ninny.

Sappho, the great Lesbian. Songs of love. Threw herself from promontory 1000 ft. into ocean. Had most beautiful cunt ever!

Indra—goddess with 100 arms. Symbol of greed or possessiveness? Or great sensuality? Not content to feel just prick and balls. Always grabbing, clutching, cuddling.

Why a poet can be inspired to write a noble or ignoble poem at sight of a fly with one wing torn off!!

Thus his ribs in remembrance of feel of left buttock sings his melancholy dirge.

Renoir, kissing canvas before beginning. Painting with brushes tied to his arms. *Une femme qui péte n'est pas morte.* A woman who farts is not dead.)

His beautiful models and hats and boats. In love with the flesh. Sensualist!

Rabelais—rebuilding walls of Paris with human cunts! But then the flies would come in swarms! *Dommage!* Pre-bidet period in France! Cunts all smelled bad!

Dogs facing opposite directions when fucking. Sometimes three dogs to one bitch.

The whore who did it fifty times a day—for almost nothing. Lips of vulva so big hung down like empty sacks! Had no feelings. Jobs lasted only 10 to 15 minutes.

6:15 P.M. Sunday 7/29/77

Dear Brenda—

The phone just rang and when I got to it there was no answer. I hope it wasn't you telling me you couldn't make it.

I have been thinking of you all day long and at the same time humming to myself the words and melodies of old songs, like

1.) "Meet Me Tonight in Dreamland"
2.) "School Days, School Days"
3.) "Roses of Picardy"

I asked Charles if he remembered any of them and he said no, he never heard of them. That made me feel really *old*. Anyway, these tunes are still rolling around in my head! I wonder if you knew any of them, though they are way before your time.

"Roses of Picardy" was a great favorite of mine. I remember weeping when I heard Edmund Burke, an Irish tenor, sing it in a London Music Hall.

Then the dreamland one, ending like this—"Meet me in Dreamland, sweet dreamy dreamland, there where my dreams come true." But the one I keep singing *now* to myself is "School Days." You probably have heard that one. I forgot two lines and made up my own:

> You were my queen in calico
> I was your bashful, barefoot beau . . .

> HENRY

●

When *Tropic of Cancer* was first published, it was the beginning of Henry Miller's new life as a celebrated writer. It was also the end of his great love affair with his wife, June Smith. Before the book was completed, she read the manuscript, and was devastated by the way Henry had portrayed their life together. She fled Paris, going into virtual seclusion in Arizona. Henry told me that he wrote letters to her apologizing and begging for forgiveness. They were returned unopened. Henry grieved, feeling she was rejecting both the artist and the man.

June, or Mona as she chose to call herself, was a fascinating woman. Henry was obsessed in his adoration of her.

They met when June was a taxi dancer. Henry was dancing with another girl, and talking about Strindberg. June came over to Henry and said that she felt as if she actually *were* Henriette, the Strindberg heroine. Henry dashed off and returned with an armful of dance tickets.

Before long June had told Henry she was the heroine in a remarkable number of Henry's favorite books, in particular Filipovna in Dostoievsky's *The Idiot,* Victoria in one of Knut Hamsun's books, and Ayesha in H. Rider Haggard's *She.* He loved her varying personas as she shifted heroines. She was a living theater.

June was taller than Henry, and he had always been insecure about being bald ever since he had lost his hair in high school: The first time she walked toward him outside the dance hall he felt awkward. But she quickly overcame his shyness. They stopped for an aperitif, walked again, and made love that night in a taxi.

She was always ready to make love to Henry anywhere, time, or place. He told me he was embarrassed and yet thrilled. It was exciting when she would mount him in a taxi, or when walking down a street, she would pull him into a *pissoir*. If they were in a park she would drag him off into the bushes, or onto a bench, or find a patch of grass. When visiting friends, such as Alfred Perles, June would often pull Henry into the nearest bedroom and seduce him.

She rarely wore underwear. But when she did, he said, she would cut the centers out of her bra cups. Around their flat, June took great pleasure in being erotic for Henry. She mopped the floor in a sexy evening dress, wore an open kimono, keeping herself as exposed as possible. Henry said he would often look up from the typewriter and get a view of June crossing her legs for his benefit. He said he liked to bathe and douche her. And he would inevitably end up in the tub with her, making love.

Henry loved her voice. Deep, guttural, and caressing, it helped make her a gifted story-teller. Henry loved the fact that she had Gypsy blood, and felt she used her whole being in telling her stories—her almond Gypsy eyes would change colors as she spoke, her graceful long hands would dance about as she created her characters.

He was fascinated that she was a dancer. She was the most sought-after woman he had ever known. He always beamed with pride whenever they would go out in public. He said everyone envied him when he was with her. He also remarked on her beautiful long legs. He said it was because she was a dancer that she had a gazelle-like gait when she walked. He said when he went with her to work he liked just to stand and watch her walk away because she was so exotic and beautiful to look at.

When I listened to Henry talk this way about her, the same nagging question kept coming back to me—but I was afraid to ask him. Finally, one night over dinner, I raised it. *Big mistake!* I had found an open wound.

I blurted out with little thought: "If you are such a truthful man, then why do you write one way and act another? I cannot understand how such an elegant, scholarly gentleman who is so charming and attentive towards women in his real life can write about women with such contempt." I wanted to know why his descriptions of lovemaking were anything but lovemaking. He seemed to be two men—the man I knew who was the "Last of the Great Romantics," and the writer who prided himself on his graphic descriptions of raw sex.

Henry responded angrily, "Why, why, why? Don't ever ask me 'why?' There is no answer to why. People do what they want to do."

I kept going, I couldn't stop at this point, even though Henry was stunned. "If you really are the free man you claim to be, how do you explain this? You portrayed June like a streetwalker, a nickel-and-dime whore, which she wasn't. Or was she? You coaxed her into marrying you, not the other way around. She supported you and loved you. If she took money from a man and gave it to you, so you could be the literary giant you are today, then *you* are the hypocrite! You *killed* June in Paris with *Tropic of Cancer!*"

He dropped his fork and almost leaped out of his wheelchair, infuriated. He told me that I didn't understand, that I had not been there at that time, and who was I to judge something that I knew nothing about. It was the first and only time I had seen him lose his temper. I hated myself for what I had said, and fled. All the way home I was in a daze. That night I wrote him a letter asking to be forgiven for hurting him.

The next day I received a special delivery letter and telegram berating me for my actions. Later that day, after I had cried so much that my eyes swelled with pain, Henry phoned me. He asked if I had gotten his letter. He apologized for sounding so cruel in the letter. He wanted me to come over for dinner so we could talk about it. I said I was sorry for ever bringing it up.

Sometime later, I was able to ask Henry to explain how his relationship with June *really* was. He said he suspected that she was unfaithful, that she was, in actuality, a fabricator.

He began to be able to talk about June with me, to finally get rid of his guilt about what she felt he did to her. And I stopped becoming June for him. He began to deal with me as Brenda.

I asked Henry if he would write me a short scene depicting their relationship. He said he'd try. And when he presented it to me, he said he hoped it would please me. As a present, I performed the play to a full audience, which included Henry.

•

Monday

Dear Brenda—

Here is the scene Your Majesty commanded last night. I hope it's suitable. Is it too short? Hope not.

As you can see, I had you in mind as well as June in writing this. Hope you don't mind. (Maybe that's what you really wanted.) It seems to answer a lot of questions, this little scene.

I do hope you find it satisfactory. Your Majesty isn't easy to please in these matters. It was dashed off in about three hours. (Perhaps it could be improved? Could you do that?)

So long now. I need a bit of a nap.

Your darling

HENRY

SCENE FROM UNFINISHED PLAY

Modest flat in big city—sparsely furnished but in good taste, *à la Japonaise!*

STELLA, the wife
HAL, the husband

Hal is a young aspiring writer who has had nothing accepted as yet. He stays home, cooks the meals, does the woman's work.

Stella, formerly an actress, about 5 years older than Hal, has sacrificed her stage career in order to help her young husband become a famous writer. She has undertaken to supply the necessary wherewithal. *How* nobody knows. She is home during day. Leaves around dinner and usually returns about 3:00 A.M.

SCENE

Hal is seated in front of machine. He has been unable to write a line all evening. Hearing her footsteps on stairs he begins to hammer the keys without making any sense.

Stella bursts in on him in fine fettle, and, seeing him at the machine, begs to read what he has written.

HAL

(Jumping up)
No, Stella, sorry I can't let you see what I've done tonight—it's no good.

STELLA

I don't care—that's what you always say. Please . . . !

HAL

(Moving her away from his table for fear she will see the nonsense he has typed out)
Oh forget about *me.* How was your night tonight? You look happy. Did you strike it rich?

STELLA

No-o, not exactly. But I met a wonderful man. What I'd call a real gentleman. He's in the advertising business. Has a wife who's an invalid. I wish you could meet him . . .

HAL

Yes, I'll meet them all some day or other, I guess. Funny how you meet so many men who are so kind to their wives. How do you manage it?

STELLA

(Taking umbrage at this last remark)
Now Hal, don't get sarcastic. You trust me, don't you?

HAL

(Quickly)
Certainly, you know that. If I didn't I'd have committed suicide long ago.

STELLA

That isn't a very kind observation.

HAL

Forgive me, I didn't mean it that way.

STELLA

(Getting irritable)
How *did* you mean it then?

HAL

(Hoping to change the subject)
You know, Stella, I never question how you spend your time of a night. If I were a jealous husband I could imagine all manner of things.

STELLA

Like what, for instance?

HAL

O, let's not go into that . . .
    (Suddenly, as if the idea had just hit him)
You know, Stella, that's what I was writing about tonight . . . not exactly, but . . .

STELLA

Go on! Sounds interesting.

HAL

(Taking the lead)
Yes, you see, I got to imagining *what* you could possibly be doing from 8:00 P.M. to 3:00 A.M. and so I began writing it, thinking of

you as a character in my book. In fact, reproducing *our* life as nearly as possible. All except that blank at night.

STELLA

I can believe you have thought the worst now and then. Most men would.

HAL

Yes, when I'm writing about a fictive character I can imagine most anything . . .

STELLA

(Interrupting)
Keep on. Tell me some more—I'm curious.

HAL

You're sure you won't get angry?

STELLA

Of course not. Don't forget I'm an actress.

HAL

That's what I fear. Actresses are known for losing their temper.

STELLA

Tell me the worst—I'm getting impatient.

HAL

O.K. Here goes. The most . . .

STELLA

(Quickly)
You didn't make me out to be a whore, I hope.

HAL

(Facetiously)
Isn't every woman a whore at bottom?

STELLA

(With acerbity)
No, every woman *ain't* a whore at bottom and you know that.

HAL

I was only joking. How could I make the woman I love out to be a whore?

STELLA

Writers can do many strange things. Besides, I do think it's possible for a man to be in love with a whore. I was the next thing to being one when we met.

HAL

Maybe it was your colorful background which made me fall in love with you.

STELLA

(Seemingly ignoring the remark)
Hal, we're forgetting what you wrote. Tell me now, how did you see me, in just what light?

HAL

To tell the truth, the first thing that came to mind was—a whore. But a very discreet, very intelligent one. That's where I began to bog down this evening. It just didn't suit you. On the other hand, I couldn't deny that it had to do with sex . . .

Stella listens with a weird smile, as if to say, "How stupid can you get?"

HAL

(Continuing)
So, the next thing comes up is to make you the mistress of a man in distress . . .

STELLA

You mean someone without balls?

HAL

Yeah—a little like that. In fact, what you told me when you came home came very near the mark.

STELLA

What do you mean?

HAL

I mean the wonderful man with the invalid wife. Needs a companion, preferably blonde, etc., etc. . . .

Stella breaks out laughing.

HAL

What's so funny? What did I say?

STELLA

It's not what you say, it's what you didn't say. You want me to be sexy, but no fucking, right? Is that just to save your face? You know it's an impossible situation.

HAL

(Breaking into laugh)
I guess you're right. I told you it was no go tonight.

STELLA

Forget what you wrote or didn't write—go on with the story right from here. Let me watch you write in your head.

HAL

(Somewhat embarrassed)
That's pretty hard to do, Stella, a writer needs privacy, you know.

STELLA

Forget all that. Just speak what's on your mind. I'll help you.

HAL

All right, I'll try.
(He pauses)

STELLA

I hope you made me attractive. I don't mean just sexually. I'm no sex-pot. Did you remember that I had been an actress—and not too bad a one?

HAL

Most of all I recalled your ability to talk.
(To himself)

That's most of what an actress does. I made you "irresistible"—how do you like that?

STELLA

That suits me fine. Go on . . .

HAL

What I stress about your talk is the way you use the language. It's a cross between a university graduate and a beauty queen. *Racy*, I'd say, like your hands and legs.

STELLA

But what am I doing all night? I'm not twiddling my thumbs, *am* I?

HAL

Of course not. You're—

STELLA

Or am I fucking my head off?

HAL

Not that either. You're fucking your head off with me, right?

STELLA

Hal, I love you. It makes me sort of slap-happy to see you in a quandary. You're usually so confident, so sure of yourself. *Or else you're a damn good actor!*

HAL

(Sensing that they are at the edge of truth)
Listen—wait a moment. Whom are we talking about—an imaginary character or the man you met tonight, as you say.
(Slight pause)
Or was it *three* months ago?

STELLA

(Calmly)
Six months, dear Hal.

HAL

(Encouraged by this piece of veracity)
So then you *are* whoring it?

STELLA

If you want to call it that!

HAL

Well, what else could you call it? It's all my fault. I should never
have allowed you to play the man's part.
    (Another pause—his face suddenly brightening)
You know something—it makes no difference at all! *I love you.* I'll
always love you! I don't care if you sleep with a thousand men.

STELLA

(Stifling a yawn and beginning to undress)
Let me be your little whore, yes?

HAL

Yes! Wonderful! I love you more than ever.
    (He begins to help her undress.)
Quick! Let's get to bed!

STELLA

No, right here on the floor.

HAL

Is that how *he* likes it?

STELLA

(To his utter amazement)
Yes!

Though slightly embarrassed, they are both relieved to put an end to the
pretense they have created ever since their marriage.

HAL

You must tell me all the things you did with him.
    (He means sexually)

STELLA

Certainly, only it will take me more than one night.
(Stops abruptly. An idea has come into her head.)
Hal, maybe we have the solution for your book. I'll tell you my
adventures with the various men I've known and you write it out.

They fall into a clinch and drop to the floor.

CURTAIN

By Henry Miller for Brenda Venus   10/25/77

Friday 10/27/77

Dearest Brenda—

How are you today, my love? It was beautiful to see you last night at
Le Cellier's. (*Folle à la messe. Molle à la fesse.* Translation goes like
this:

Crazy at mass
Soft in the ass)

Your friend Charals Haagen was delightful. Weren't you two ever in
love? I should imagine you could love a man like that! Or am I all
wrong?

Tony and Sandi are rearranging all the books in the house. The
place looks a mess. (Has to be done in true Virgo style.)

I was searching for a pair of shoes to wear in case it rains, as I must
not get my feet wet. Have six or seven pair in closet, but none fit me
any more. My feet have spread, I guess, from wearing these white
snookers.

You mentioned last night about health value of eating animal
organs—especially the heart of most animals. I wonder what the *human*
heart tastes like? You know the stories about a king getting even with his
unfaithful wife? He has the lover killed and his heart served up to her at
dinner. She remarks how well it tastes and the king rejoins, "No wonder, it's your lover's heart!"

Strange they have never made choice bits of the sexual organs. I
would think the vagina would be delicious. (Not the prick, however—
too much muscle!)

Have a good week-end, my dear, dear Brenda. You were so wonderful last night.

HENRY

Je t'embrasse mille fois et te baise dans ma tête.

•

Henry's eighty-sixth birthday was December 26, 1977. I sent him a letter in which I told him that I felt I had changed since knowing him. I told him that he had taken me down a path of trust, faith, and love, and I was happy that I had followed.

•

THE DAY!

Saturday

Beloved Brenda!

It came at noon today, your wonderful, wonderful letter! I read it with tears in my eyes. My God, how beautifully you express your thoughts and feelings. Sometimes, as I read you, I begin to tremble—I ask myself—Can she possibly mean me? Who am I? Who is this Henry Miller? And so on and so forth. It doesn't seem possible that one person could arouse such love, such adulation and adoration. Brenda, Brenda, it is my turn to be mute. Before such loving eloquence I am tongue-tied.

You ask if I see it all in your eyes. Indeed I do, my dear one. Everything is written in your eyes. *And in all of you.* You vibrate from every pore, even if the mouth be shut. You know, I get up frequently during the night, turn on the light, and look at your photo, your image on the book shelf. It always spells not only beauty, but purity, integrity, confidence.

I keep thinking of you as a flower from the deep South, with such a wondrous fragrance, and a seeming fragility. Actually, you are strong as a tiger—and as dangerous when angered, I fear. My sight is dimming now. I have been writing without glasses. Hearing from you, I imagine I can do anything.

Yes, dearest, dearest Brenda, it is only because of *you* that I am alive today. I know it better than anyone.

Sandi always asks lovingly about you. Val asks if she can come visit soon. I do wish you could spend a few days in our little cabin. You know, you could fly to Monterey and back. Val could meet you and drive you down the coast. Think about it.

I love you, love you, love you. You are everything to me . . . When I think of your Dad I sing to myself, "Yankee Doodle Dandy"—tho' that's not exactly the tune Southerners like. But then I don't know that great rebel song very well, tho' it makes my blood stir when I hear it. "*Look away, look away* . . ."

Don't look away, dear Brenda. Look straight at everything. Look it all in the eye, good and bad. God be with you!

Your

HENRY

P.S. Let's hope I live long enough to do a commercial with you, or better yet, *for you*.

●

Two men named Little John Chesko and Richard Young had asked Henry if we could tape a wine commentary in Henry's house. When Richard and Little John arrived with their crew they found Henry in an ill temper. I suspect he hadn't slept well the night before and all those people trying to set up their equipment was too much to bear.

Henry was supposed to speak frankly and spontaneously, which is exactly what he did, but about everything *except* the wine! Everything that was put before him he would taste and sharply criticize, saying, "What is this? This chicken is not so tender, by the way." Or, "I'm not fussy, but this is a complete disappointment. This is pitiful!" And the remaining dinner he felt was even more abominable. According to Henry, nothing was right.

I kept encouraging Henry to say something about the various wines he was sipping, but he pointedly ignored me while regaling the camera with his powers as a raconteur. Finally, after he could no longer ignore my pestering him for *some* comment, he tasted a glass and said, "Yeah. Hmmm . . ." And that was it!

When we looked at the tape a few days later, we saw that although it was definitely not commercial material, it was so funny that Little John and Richard decided to use it as part of a documentary on Henry.

•

1978

•

At eighty-six Henry was experiencing an increasing amount of random aches and pains. He continued to work hard almost every day. His will to live simply overpowered his physical problems.

•

1/13/78

Dear, dear Brenda—

I have been answering letters for about 3 hours and haven't finished yet. But I feel you ought to get one that is not an Answer but an Incentive to Answer. I think of you between all the lines I write. I just answered the editor of a Hindu mag in New Delhi who asked to whom or what I was indebted for my renown. Impossible to answer briefly but I did, saying Nietzsche, Emma Goldman, Swami Vivekananda, and Prince Kropotkin (Russian anarchist, author of *Bread*) had influenced me greatly, but that I had not hoped to change the world by my work. How foolish? Isn't God's handiwork good enuf for us?

What letters! What requests! You can't imagine! This, of course, is a hangover from Xmas and Birthday mail. I got *one dollar* out of it all— for return postage.

Where are you today, my valiant wanderer? Are you still in good fighting spirit? Any chance of employment soon? Keep a stiff upper lip—and a stiff lower one, too. Though not the too low one. That should be soft, flexible, vulnerable at all times. I sing your praises softly to myself. I hug and caress you, whisper in your ear (sweet nothings!), etc., etc. Don't overlook the et ceteras—very important. Remember, whatever spurts from my lips is not coarse but *raffinée*. Even the crude obscenities. All part of God's handiwork. Like you and me.

So long now. I need a nap. Even prone I'll be thinking of you—*all*ways. Bye-bye for a while.

> Your chickadee
>
> HENRY

> March 4, 1978
> 1:00 A.M.

Dearest Brenda—

Can't sleep. Took Anacin and Valium—no go. Can't get you out of my mind. Where are you? What hinders you from writing or telephoning? Is anything vitally amiss? Have you fallen out of love—or into a new one?

I miss you, miss you, miss you. Didn't realize how dependent I was on your presence, your love. Now I am in a trough—not yet of utter despair, but of sheer mystery. I don't seem to get any silent messages from you or else the cosmic waves have been too battered by the recent storms.

Yet—I thought the powers of the mind (or heart) could overcome such obstacles. I still believe so. I expect the miraculous from you, of you. I am sure, despite everything, that wherever you are you are thinking of me.

I trust you are not in a hospital or clinic. Even so I imagine you could get word to me.

Brenda, come alive! Talk to me—over the ether waves if need be. But don't leave me in utter silence and solitude!

> I love you, love you.
>
> HENRY

> April 19, 1978

My dear, dear Brenda—

I lay in bed again all day today, trying to cure pain in my back. Pain has diminished somewhat, but is still there. Haven't done a stroke of work, naturally, but just dreamed the time away.

Thus, I went over your whole life, as you have chosen to tell me it. Some parts are vague, others very vivid. I even gave you another name, as if I were relating the story of your life—"Guerlaine" (after the perfume.) First I wanted to make it Ghislaine (an Arthurian-sounding name) but then I recalled that that's the name of Durrell's freshly divorced wife who, he says, gave him a very bad time.

I wonder, if you had the choice, what you would call yourself!

Also, it seems to me you told me you were writing a script. Are you putting yourself in it, and, if so, do you make it true to nature or do you give yourself extraordinary qualities and virtues? I am curious. I think it almost impossible to be wholly truthful about one's self, even though telling the rotten side of oneself often adds a certain piquancy to the portrait. What say?

I hope you received my rather lengthy letter today! All day I have had the notion that you were going to walk in on me and stand before the bed in utter silence until I *felt* your presence. How very wonderful that entrance always is! Few women know how to avail themselves of it.

Ever read Mark Twain? The other day his grandson made me an honorary member of the Mark Twain Society. Which reminds me of a day in Mississippi when I was standing on the grounds of some famous plantation on the banks of the river and my companion (a Southerner) whispered in my ear, "Mark Twain used to pass by here in his steamer." How come I missed Hattiesburg? And you?

Signing off now—with all my love and tenderness.

HENRY

BRENDA VENUSIANA!

From the milky globes
To the milky cleft
The Givenchy route
Reminiscences of earlier days in the womb
Solitary confinement
With all the trimming
Disturbed occasionally
Knocked from one corner to another
During the nuptial orgies
But ever secure, ever serene,

Just waiting for the signal to out
Impatient to cut the navel cord
The dull, passive existence
Without love, without sex, without . . .
Waiting for Scorpio to round the Heavens
And open the door to life
A life unbelievable, undeniable . . .
Here she comes—Brenda
Daughter of Love, shimmering
In her veil of sex
Astride her Aurora Borealis
Made to be adored
Worshipped, taken again and again
The Venus of Love.

HENRY MILLER

●

He had a great passion for saints, especially St. Francis of Assisi and Cabeza de Vaca, who in 1528 was a lieutenant in the service of the king of Spain on an ill-starred expedition to Florida. He, two other Spaniards, and a Moor were the only survivors. For eight grueling years they wandered around North America performing miracles of healing for the Indians, who became their brothers.

De Vaca was a hero to Henry. He would tell me this particular story over and over, repeating it so that I would memorize the words of a man who was once a warrior and a conqueror. "I shall teach the world how to conquer by gentleness, not by slaughter."

And Henry wanted me to memorize a saying from St. Francis: "As much as a man is before God, so much is he and no more."

The significance of these heroes, for Henry, was that they were examples of men stripped of everything and obliged to act out every moment of their lives in the sight of God. This is how he explained it. Henry related very closely to these great men in

the quest for the truth. He looked at all human beings as both
sensualist and spiritualist. For him, saints were the most
powerful expression of both these aspects of man because they
struggled the most passionately with them.

•

April 25, 1978

My darling, my beloved Brenda—

I have had a stamped addressed envelope on my desk (to you) these
last 72 hours, always hoping to catch time to write you. My mind was
full of so many things—*censorable* ones too—and now it has all drib-
bled away, answering the many, many who write me about this and
that.

Giles Henley (in England) sent a letter enclosing a British T.V. mag
with an article by Lawrence Durrell about his film visit to Egypt. I was
swept away by it. (Mia Farrow is in one of the photos with him.) Durrell
is apparently writing a new book about Egypt—Egypt after six years
absence. He writes so simply, limpidly, feelingly—especially for place
and color. Well, you'll see. (I wonder if you ever read his *Alexandria
Quartet*—made him famous as the *Tropics* did me.) But I won't push
you to read even the greatest masterpiece of modern times because you
are in the throes of creativity yourself . . .

To change the tune . . . What I had wanted to elaborate on 48
hours or so ago was the odd tendency (on my part) to be aroused sexually at the thought of you being a saint, even in embryo. Mulling it
over, I recall seeing pictures of St. Anthony in the desert, going through
the tortures of hell because of his sex desires and images. You see, when
the saints got horny, so to speak, it wasn't like with ordinary men's
desires. The saints were extraordinary beings, with extraordinary appetites—and the chief one was the pleasures of the flesh . . .

Thus, thinking back on your early life, that girl friend in Hattiesburg
who was a little older than you and perhaps a little more *lascivious*, I got
to thinking of you as you are today, so pure, so statuesque, and so
terribly, passionately exciting in a low key. Every time your dress flew
open to reveal a patch of alabaster, every time my hand rested near the
Delta of Venus, I could feel the heat emanating from it. Pure as I am
with you, yet your image is ever most exciting. You are like the
"*Madonna of Sex,*" if there be such a creature. What a silent passionate
language we share. And against what backdrop! Sleazy L.A., or the

booth at Imperial Gardens, or the front seat of your car. Yes, all these are heavenly spots too—perhaps only for brief moments, like when you forget (?) yourself or what. All of which only excites me the more. How could I attack the *Primavera*? How could I dare fondle the delta of Venus or the noble globes above? Rather would I lick your feet, kiss your glowing backside! Do you see what I mean?

In other words, Henry Miller the saint, the wise man, is even more interested in your physical attributes. *Comme il faut!* I know you will forgive these rash thoughts. But tell me do you ever have the like as regards *yours truly*?

That's what I wanted to get off my chest. I hug you and kiss you everywhere.

> Your devoted and
> slightly delirious lover,
>
> HENRY

4/25/78

Dear, dear Brenda—

Another day of exhausting mail. Bert Mathieu sent a special delivery with about 20 pages of handwriting and a long letter from his new publisher asking my help—literary and graphic wise. It will take days to answer and decide what to ask for my services.

Seems every day brings new problems. My sight is giving way. And each day I have an envelope ready to mail you—but no letter!

Fuck it all! *You come first*. I must remember that. Am wondering if you received the "scorcher" I wrote yesterday. Maybe to you it will not seem so "scorching." You are more sophisticated than I, I do believe. I am really quite an innocent one—an angel with *clipped wings*. (That was title of first book I wrote—long since lost.) Curious, eh? Of course I did not include *An Angel*. Perhaps I didn't even think of one—unless unconsciously.

About saints, both male and female. Somehow they are always associated in my mind with fierce *sexual* desires. That's why their struggle with the flesh was so *"heroic."* You follow me?

And I, in my old age, I who thought I had solved that problem, find it flaring up again. *But,* I started out to write you about writing, *your* writing and writing in general.

One of the first things you have to recognize, if you are a *serious* artist, is that art has no rules. Everything else under the sun has, but not art. With art *you are free*, provided you follow the bidding of your heart and not your mind. (Do you know anything about the Dadaist movement? It was *something*. Unfortunately it didn't *take* with the public. It had to do with "clowns and angels," idiots, traitors, scoundrels. It was like becoming a child again, but *an unruly one*. I always remember them putting you in a convent in Biloxi. Today you have learned a bit of compromise, but one still senses the rebel in you. And a lot of other things, too.)

However you manage to suppress the sexual drive is still a mystery to me.

Back to the writing biz . . . Brenda, literature is like music, painting, or any other art. You have to be yourself all the time. That won't mean early profits. On the contrary, you will find all the snares and traps that you have in T.V. With everything, whether art, love, or what not, the element of *chance* plays a certain role, a rather big one, I would say. Learn to cultivate chance, to spot it at a glance. Don't besiege your astrologer. Get to know your own heart and mind. Follow your instincts. And remember (I'm sure you do!) that *success* demands sacrifices. Success, though it seems like the goal, is your greatest enemy. I would say, "Don't try to be Number 1, just be *whatever you are. Be it fully and constantly.*"

Well, there you are. Sounds a little like the Sermon on the Mount. You know, tho' I am not a Christian or Jew or Mohammedan, certain things (of a religious nature) make great sense to me. Your early sainthood has not wholly left you. May it preserve you and not be a curse and a stumbling block. As I see you, you are pure gold. Better, you are of some divine elixir mixed with clay. You don't need to worry about "getting there." You *are* there now, already and forever.

Enuf! I am half blind with all I have read today. See you Thursday I hope—for Fuji Gardens. Fuji is from *Fuji yama*! Cheers, joy, sensuality, and sublimity all in one!

Your angelic worshipper

HENRY

LETTER TO BELOVED

At love letters you are the queen! Incomparable—*Ausgezeichnet* (Extraordinary).

My dear one, I have been wondering all day (between letters) where you have been spending the day. Hopefully in the arms of Neptune, not some movie star.

I see you in the water, one with Neptune, letting his friendly waves kiss every part and parcel of you. And you reveling in it—awash with glee, glamour, and glycerine. How wonderful if only I could swim beside you or even on your back! When you told me you couldn't wear the beautiful Japanese blouse Paul gave you I was absolutely astonished. Skin too tender. Yet it takes bruises, scratches, kicks, broken bones and what not. You are an *oxymoron* physically. A daredevil to boot. I always dream of how magnificent it would be just to lie beside you one night. Like a dream come true. And so it's true, you love me. Always have— from eternity. It's so unbelievably wonderful. I could hug myself. You have changed somewhat since I know you. Your true colors are shining forth more boldly; you are getting more familiar with me, so to speak, though that's a droll way of putting it. You wear well. You seem immune to most feminine susceptibilities. Not that you are mannish. No, but you know your own mind, your own habits, weaknesses, and strengths. And you are usually in excellent good humor. Usually soft to touch—and *très touchable*.

I was talking at table about my first glimpse of ancestral home: Minden am Weser, Germany. How when I saw this birthplace of my father's father I said to myself, "How could he ever have left this beautiful village for America!" (But both grandfathers left Germany rather than be made into military robots.) And their grandchildren have followed suit. Allah be praised!

My dear, I trust you will forgive me if I stop here. I am really pooped. All I will add is that I love you more and more each day. Never get enough of you, my tender, elegant queen of the harem. Keep reading *Disenchanted*. You will grow with it and deepen and become even more what you already are.

Your beloved

HENRY

Saturday June 23, 1978

Dearest Brenda,

Since you seem to believe I can write poetry I am taking the liberty of sending you another. I wrote it last night after telephoning you.

It was inspired by Cendrars' *Pâques à New York*—"Easter in New York," when he was starving here—and I at the same time, but not knowing of him then. When I think of holidays (like July 4th coming up) I must tell you that ever since I became of age I was penniless every holiday in the year, Christmas, New Year's, Easter, Labor Day, Mother's Day, Father's Day, etc., etc. Only in the last ten years, one might say, have I lived like a normal human being. That is, with 3 meals a day. Now it's just *two*—of my own volition.

Be careful I *don't eat you* some day when I am hungry again.

I miss you body and soul very, very much. It will be a treat to see you Sunday. Let's gorge ourselves!

Love and kisses and all that it implies—forever and ever!

HENRY

June 22, 1978

IN MEMORY OF BLAISE CENDRARS

O Jesus, if you are not a myth
If you once inhabited this earth
And shook the planet with your purity and gentleness
If you still exist among the dead
If there is any magic left in your possession
Give heed to these miserable citizens of a rotten world
A world of power and violence named America
Give heed to the poor blacks, the downtrodden Mexicans
The artists who struggle in vain
Say there is a tomorrow
Just as there was a yesterday
Say more—sing of eternity
An eternity not of salvation
But of life, life to the utmost
Wherein power no longer has meaning

Nor piety nor weakness
But creativity in whose hands the artist rests
Say that he can and will bring about a resurrection
Not of the dead but of the everlasting spirit
Which gives the birds to sing
The flowers to dazzle us
The sky and stars to bewilder
Give it all back to us intact
As it came from the hands of the Creator!

Henry Miller

9:00 P.M. Monday

Dear Brenda—

One of the words Mathieu wrote out on a big card before he left was—ENANTIODRÒMOS or the process whereby a thing changes into its opposite—like love to hate, beauty to ugliness, etc.

Since going to bed at 8:30 I am wide awake, my mind racing. Started with musicians—composers. Those I like and those I don't care for, such as Bach, Beethoven and Mozart. Awakened memories of Ravel's "Gaspard de la Nuit," one of my great favorites, like Hamsun's *Mysteries*. In bed I got to thinking who was the greatest personality in European history—Gilles de Rais, the white knight who saved Joan of Arc at the Battle of Orleans, and then after her burning at the stake, turned into a monster, violating children and murdering them (depopulating whole villages of their youth). When found guilty in court, he got on his knees in all his finery and begged the audience (made up mostly of parents of children he had murdered) and begged them to *pray for his soul!*

Then the most wonderful man of Europe—St. Francis of Assisi (who included atheists as well as pious ones among his kind).

And the greatest work of art, in my opinion, the Triptych called "The Mystic Lamb" by Van Eyck in the Cathedral of Ghent, Belgium.

But enough! My head is still reeling with names and deeds! Good night, my angel.

HENRY

June 30, 1978

And now my Sicilian beauty, we get down to *you*, the one and only, the future star, the dazzler! Just got off a long, *sensible* (feeling) letter to an old Paris friend who sent me a little book with reproductions of his paintings and texts by me, André Breton, et alia. I was very moved. He wrote he lost his Una (his wife) last year—another *long* marriage. Says he feels lonely and works *less*, but lives in a mill in the Champagne region of France. This after living like a louse most of his life, fighting for a crust of bread, a hallway to sleep in (on bare floor), someone to buy a painting, acting as guide to tourists, swallowing so much dreadful shit.

His paintings are *not* of our time—but recollection of his youth in Bessarabia (Roumania). Pictures of rape, murder, drunkenness, insanity, God knows what all. I reminded him of my visit with June (1927 or 28) to Czernowitz, Roumania on the Russian border. The flies so thick that at meal time two sons with fans kept brushing the flies away from our food. Also the lunatics, idiots, whores, greedy merchants galore. Memories, memories!!! But then I told him when he feels lonely to think of the stars, of rabbits, of field mice, of lice and cockroaches and grass and flowers—all a part of the universe with us. But we never hear of their suffering or their loneliness.

Then I told him how lucky I was to have *you*—how incredible, such a God-given blessing. Yes, dear Brenda, every letter you write me only makes me think how more and more marvelous it all is. You are the light of my life—from crown to toenail. Every part of you is precious to me, including those which are "défendus"!! You say you dream of me quite often—how, in what way, I wonder?

I feel so close to you now that the holidays will keep us apart a little longer. Sometimes I could just undress you and lick you from head to toe. In my sleep I run my hands over the curves in your physique— what a thrill! Like being proficient in runs at the piano. (Czerny's finger exercises.)

I hope you are staying fit and that *you eat enough* each day. Seems to me you are starving yourself. Where do you get all your energy? Surely not simply from shutting off the sex machine? (Did you notice that in Hindu thinking one gets great strength from sex without ejaculation?) Curious that sex too can be a way to God or liberation! Do you remember Hesse's book *Siddartha*? Do you remember what Siddartha answers when his would-be employer asks, "What good to me are you, a forest monk?" And S. replies, "I know three things: I can think, I can wait, and I can do without."

The last is the great one. If we can master that, we've made it, *n'est-ce pas?*

You've got it all made in advance, my darling. It's just like you are waiting to try on a new suit! Hold to it! Never give up except to *rest!* I love you beyond all words!

> Be well and take care!
>
> HENRY

August 1st, 1978

Darling, darling—

I have to write you immediately! Your letter was magnificent—*all I expected of you!* Simple, direct, true, sincere—and such a great love. You put me, the writer, to shame. You write with your heart's blood, I with ink.

I can imagine everything you hint at in the dream sequence. But the day visions are really hallucinatory.

Take good, good care of yourself, my precious one. It would be overwhelming if anything were to happen to you now.

In another view . . . when I got up to go to the desk, I felt the back of my upper leg. It felt so strong I couldn't believe it was me. Even in the matter of limbs there is a connection. We are two physio-spiritual Siamese twins.

That card was a *Loulou!* You are a Renoir in his loveliest period. Needless to add—I am mad about you.

> All my love and affection
>
> HENRY

P.S. This sounds so trivial besides yours—*but the love is there!*

Aug. 2, 1978

Precious lovely Brenda—

Will be seeing you tomorrow, I hope. Have just reread your letter. There was a word you asked about—*emanate,* I believe. One could say of you that an unnamable perfume *emanates* from you. In other words, *comes from* or *is given* off. Your body is all honey and perfume—and freedom and seduction and temptation and God knows what all. You are made of essences—such as are used in very sacred temples which nevertheless have devotees who are temple whores. They give one a "religious fuck"—can you picture that? When you speak of going to the convent as a girl it seems to me there was a trace of sensuality in that noble desire of yours. The ritual of the church is sometimes very erotic. And that's how you are—a virgin bathed in sensuality. That's the "chemistry" you mention in your letter. You are like a flower about to open and fully opened at the same time. (Your clitoris is always active.) On rereading you today I get the impact of your letter not only in my affectionate areas but in the genitals, too.

I must interrupt here to tell you I awoke about 4:00 A.M. this morning, with a strong feeling that I was going to die. Some few hours later I discovered the reason for this sombre thought. My heart doctor had written a letter to my divorce lawyer (at the latter's request) explaining to the court why I could or should not make an appearance in court—for the final decree—Aug. 7th. He gave such a picture of my condition that the after-effect hit me at 4:00 A.M. What clinched it was his postscript—"Nor is there any hope for any improvement in his health." (That *was for the judge!*) But it sank deep into my unconscious, I guess.

And as if to combat it I got to thinking of you and how healthy I seem ever since we fell in love. And the next thing you know I had an erection—and you were holding it in your hand—pleasurably. *Alors, c'est le* chemistry, *n'est-ce pas?*

I will stop here before the page begins to smoke!!! I love you with an unholy love such as Heloise had for Abelard. Do you remember her letter—"Would that I loved my God as I do you!"

HENRY

8/8/78

Brenda darling—

I hope you will forgive me but I am on the verge of writing you a letter which may displease you. I am going to sleep on it again before I write it. It's about sex. I just can't contain myself any longer. I may sound either like a teenager or else a "dirty old man." You once said I could say or do anything I wished—you would never be offended. I hate putting you to the test. My love hasn't altered in any way—just blossomed out in this mad sexual direction—as a result of your provocation, god-like beauty, and sensibility.

I pray you will understand and forgive me, even if I overstep the limits. Then again, I may *not* write. I may suppress it all and surrender to utter chastity.

Your beloved

HENRY

P.S. Maybe you could answer me in your dreams??

Darling Brenda—

I'm dead tired. Would love to go back to bed and continue the dream I had last night—one of the most vivid and most thrilling of my long life.

It was of *us*. We were at somebody's home and we were lying on a broad couch, in our clothes. There were a half dozen people, a few yards away, making merry but not seeming to be aware of us, at least, not bothering us.

We were asleep or half asleep or pretending to be asleep—hard to tell. I recall opening my eyes now and then to look at you and you always looked as if you were blissfully asleep, but I know instinctively you weren't. You were pretending to be asleep so that I could continue my depredations. You had on a black, very thin dress, and absolutely nothing beneath it. You looked as beautiful and innocent as in those first photos you sent me—of just your head. I had an arm around and under you and, because your dress had gotten disarranged my own hand was fastened to one of your bare buttocks. You never made a move to dislodge it.

For an endless time it seemed the other hand was very slowly, very delicately, very discreetly, maneuvering to touch your cunt. It hardly moved; just inched its way along till it came to a thicket of hair, like a Scottish sporran. In the midst of this jungle, of course, was your cunt which I was trying to connect with.

I dwell on the slowness and the maneuvering because that was what made the situation so delicious. At times I would seem to wake, saying to myself, "This is incredible, I must be dreaming," and I would go back deeper into the dream and still nearer that cleft which my finger was searching for. And now, more than ever, I had to be cautious, careful you wouldn't suddenly awaken and scream—"What the hell do you think you are doing?" (Like sometimes when we come back from the restaurant, you run off in a hurry, saying, "I've got to go home," as if you had overstayed your time or as if someone (a lover?) was waiting your return.)

Meanwhile, in fooling around, the sensation of daring to handle you this way increased my emotion *and* my desire to take you—in that dream-like state.

There came the crucial moment where my finger did part the lips and pushed them apart. I was by now completely beside myself. You hadn't moved the fraction of an inch, your eyes were still closed, your expression serene or angelic and what a cunt I felt—finally with two or three fingers. It was extremely moist, soft as velvet and, though your body remained motionless, your cunt was very alive, very active, very very seductive. I remember actually coming awake, then deliberately replunging into the dream, saying to myself—"Make the most of it!"

Suddenly my prick, which may have been slumbering like a snail all the while, suddenly it stiffened and hurt at the same time, because the erection came so all at once, as it were. Now came the most touching moment of all. Dare I insert my pride or would that definitely bring you to your senses. I began by only allowing myself to enter the vestibule. Then, since you made no move, I decided to plunge—and plunge I did. Now your body reacted. You arched your back so as to permit full entry and you almost imperceptibly began to move back and forth in the true rhythm of intercourse.

Just when I was about to come we were awakened by our friends who had just discovered us and told that it was late and everyone was leaving.

I remember how you uncunted with a sigh and a very sweet wet kiss, saying as if under your breath, "Too bad, too bad. Just when it was going right." Your words astonished me. What! My Brenda talking this way? Then she does love to fuck! So that, my dear Brenda, was the gist of it. I hope you enjoy it in the reading as much as I did in the dreaming of it. I am now going back to bed in the hope of recapturing the mood, the scene, the ambiance. I will try to dream of Semiramis, the queen who conquered all Europe and parts of Asia. Defeated eventually by the Hindus, else she would have conquered the then known world!!! Which is what I know you secretly want to do with your talent, not your cunt. But this latter thing is not to be ignored or despised, seeing as how it affords us so much unbelievable and guiltless joy. What say you! O my Queen?

Here once again and always in all my love, reverence and devotion.

HENRY

Thursday Eve 9/15/78

Dear loved one,

Got out of bed to pen a few words to you. Can't sleep. Am hoping Charles or someone will deliver this to you tomorrow together with the cane.

It's wonderful to hear you can put your foot down, but it hurts me to think how it must hurt you to do that little thing. Hence the cane.

I broke the ice today and made two water colors—won't know for a day or two if I really like them. I could have made two more, if I had two more pads. It's always an adventure to start creating after you have lain fallow for a while. You get the feeling of what a shower does to a dry flowerbed.

Darling, do take it easy with that bad foot. Don't be reckless! Don't move too fast, and above all, don't drive yet! Sorry to talk to you this way, but I know how impetuous you are.

Do you know that Ionesco of the Absurd Theatre is in town? Did you ever see any of his plays? The one they are giving now is one of his least interesting—*Rhinoceros. The Chairs* is marvelous, but they seldom play it.

I met him one afternoon at my publisher's home in the suburbs of Paris. He's a Roumanian Jew, rather humorous and a good raconteur—but shy about talking theatre.

Today, I had a good letter from Isaac Singer—think I told you already.

Am I boring you?

Let's talk about *you.* How lovely, how beautiful, how full of grace and charm. How bewitching! How unique! Irving Stettner was in Atlanta and New Orleans recently, trying to sell his *Stroker.* Said it was enchanting the way storekeepers and clerks talked. He was absolutely charmed. Sandi bought two of his water colors—very poetic. But he looks emaciated, hollow chested, hump backed. Knows his way around—no money for cabs, took buses all the time and walked. A lovable guy.

Tomorrow night (Friday), is the Ali-Spinks fight. Ali said yesterday, "Just think—seats are $200 apiece. All those white folks shelling out that kinda money to see two niggers fight!" I sure hope he wins. He's the most spectacular guy in the whole world. A nigger who refused to take the white man's shit. Bravo! Even a Southerner has to like him. And when he refers to the prophet Muhammad he always says "Muhammad the Arabian" as opposed to Muhammad Ali.

Well, I'm rambling. Cause I miss being with you, touching you, inhaling your fragrance. Or should I say, as the French do of their fine wines—"your bouquet."

Whatever the bouquet that you receive tomorrow I hope you like it. Wish I could deliver it in person. Had a strong image today of being *chez vous* and you lying in bed and me bending over you and kissing you. Very real, very intense.

Enuf now. Guess you're sound asleep. Dream deep and far and high!

All my love

HENRY

Thursday 9/16/78

Dearest Brenda—

I'm trying out a new pair of reading glasses but so far don't see much difference between these and the old ones. Irving Stettner sent me a book of American place names and I have been looking up places in it like Biloxi, Pascagoula, Pensacola, Monongahela, etc. If it happens to be an Indian name all he says is "derived from an Indian tribal name"—doesn't always say what the meaning of the Indian word is. I looked up Hattiesburg—named after the wife of a man named Hattie Hardy, I believe—town founded in 1880—not so long ago.

Stettner wrote me on getting back to N.Y. He found the photocopy I sent him of your water color. He raved about it. Am almost tempted to send you his letter. He certainly is an appreciative guy.

Aside from your beauty I felt last night how strong you are, both physically and morally. How quickly you recover from this or that. *And* how even tempered you are. I don't think I'd ever want to see you fly into a rage. Have you ever noticed how ugly people look when angry? When *I* lose my temper I feel I have been untrue to myself. But there are people who know how to provoke one—how to deal with them is an eternal problem. Certainly "turning the other cheek" is not the answer. Nor "fighting fire with fire." The masters of Karate seem to know best. They either laugh or walk away without a word. If attacked they go chop-chop and their opponent is out of the picture. But primarily Karate teaches peace at any price. But only the strong, the seasoned ones can act this way. What do you say?

You asked me last night if I thought things came to you when you stopped trying. I can repeat yes, because things are always trying to reach us, but it is we (through our ignorance) who block these efforts on the part of God, destiny, or what you will. Faith *is* the great thing. Faith even when everything seems to be going wrong. Faith then especially. (This great woman Mary Baker Eddy was no fool. Faith may be useless in curing pimples and the like, but it works for the things which matter.)

Does *everything* matter? Yes! The little things are often more important than the seeming big things. Do you follow me? If we had more faith we would not push so hard, we would be more confident, more *serene*. And to my mind serenity is greater than happiness. Happiness is a much over-rated word. Joy is the thing—or bliss. That 7th Heaven feeling. Agreed?

Why am I rambling on like this? To teach myself a lesson, I guess. We sure got home fast last night. It was only 9:00 P.M. when I was taking off my clothes and you were already on the way home.

Well, enuf. Take care of your footsie and just be yourself!

Love in excelsis!

HENRY

Sept. 29, 1978

My beloved Brenda—

Since rereading your *wonderful* letter last night I seem to have traversed several worlds. First, I wrote a reply to your letter (in my head), exhausting myself thoroughly. I hardly slept a wink all night. I woke up and imagined you preparing for your trip. I thought of Sunday and how I would miss you, but glad I had suggested an extra day's vacation. And in between I thought of your fractured arch and how reckless you are with it. I feel the hurt every time you put your left foot down.

Lying abed today I recalled your exclamation at the door, when we embraced. You kept repeating—"How good you feel!" This stuck in my crop and early this morning it dawned on me *why* you were so enthusiastic! Because I was almost naked and we have never touched that way. It was flesh to flesh—and you got the full effect of it. Strangely, I had no erotic thoughts at the moment. So happy was I just to see you alive and sparkling. But on reflection I recall now the feel of your left buttock and the right teat (by accident).

Fini tout cela. Turn the page.

Today over my cup of tea (lunch) I picked up a book Sara left for me to read—it was a photo-biography of Hermann Hesse whom you have read, I believe. I sat there without glasses examining one photo after another. The man's whole life paraded before my eyes—all the places he had lived, his many, many friends (Freud, Rilke, Carl Jung). Then I began to read his own Preface to the book and was utterly entranced. So much resembled my own life. For one thing, his inability to adapt to the world, his hatred of teachers and preachers, his rebelliousness, his seemingly futile searching and seeking, until he had written his first book. (With me it was my fourth book, *Tropic of Cancer.*) He even gives his astrological signs and like myself, remarks that he had a favorable Jupiter.

But above and beyond all these facts and coincidences, I was plunged into the world of culture, the *real* culture! I relived my whole life, with all its sorrows, miseries, mishaps, good luck, great friendships, broken loves, father and son relations, etc., etc. I thought of some of my forgotten favorite writers, like Romain Rolland, Oswald Spengler, the author of *Against the Grain*, the Russian authors—all of them, Havelock Ellis, Sherwood Anderson (*The Triumph of the Egg*), etc., etc. Hesse, more than most authors I read, was deeply involved in the world of culture (*Kultur*, as the Germans call it). He was not only a rebel but a fighter, a crusader, a traveler in mind and body, a man who loved life. (German song comes to mind—"Who loves not wine, woman, and song, remains a fool his whole life long.")

And this brings me to remembrances of the *Saengerbund* or Singing Society to the meetings of which my parents dragged me when only 7 or 8 years of age. How well I remember these few hundred men and women singing in chorus, passionately, lovingly, tenderly all those songs whose words I could not understand. Like some giant organ playing. And then washing it down with big mugs of beer. An almost religious feeling about it.

And then Big Sur—coming there shortly after my Greek experience. I, who had never touched a hoe or a spade in my life, suddenly have to clear away a jungle of poison oak, dig trenches to get at their roots, raise vegetables and fruit trees. I, a Brooklyn boy, but now a poet, about to undergo two more unhappy marriages. Beautiful and crazy.

And now, a man of 87 madly in love with a young woman who writes me the most extraordinary letters, who loves me to death, who keeps me alive and in love (a perfect love for the first time), who writes me such profound and touching thoughts that I am joyous and confused as only a teenager could be. But more than that—grateful, thankful, lucky. Do I really deserve all the beautiful praises you heap on me? You cause me to wonder exactly who I am, do I really know who and what I am? You leave me swimming in mystery. For that I love you all the more. I get down on my knees, I pray for you, I bless you with what little sainthood is in me. May you fare well, dearest Brenda, and never regret this romance in the midst of your young life. We have been both blessed. We are not of this world. We are of the stars and the universe beyond.

Long live Brenda Venus! God give her joy and fulfillment and love eternal!

HENRY

Thursday   10:45 P.M.

Dearest, darling, glorious Brenda—

It's just a few minutes ago that we talked over the phone. So wonderful of you to call me. Bless your dear heart!

Still I feel we did not come out with all that was on our minds. I used guarded language again, out of respect, say I. But is it? I know you can read my mind and I feel I can yours too. Why not admit the truth? Didn't you feel like you wanted to hear me say, "I feel I could fuck you to death"?

That *cinq à sept* (five to seven) time in Paris is usually connected with sex. One goes to the café ostensibly for an aperitif, but actually at that time the whole city is swimming in sex (along with H.M. and his sexy narratives).

Yes, dear Brenda, though it is the absolute truth what I said over the phone—about chastity and a higher level of love and all that, nevertheless the opposite is also true, that more and more I want to fuck you, get inside that gorgeous figure. Looking at you tonight was like gazing at a Hindu goddess, one from a temple of Love, where there are prostitutes in the service of God or Krishna or whomever. Where there is no sense of sin, adultery, or evil. Where all is one.

And you are that one, that all in all, inspiring lust, chastity, beauty, courage, recklessness. You have *actually* become more noble these last days. Strange, too, because you are actually dealing in money matters, you are in business! (But not monkey business.)

Oh Brenda, my dear one, my only one, I hope I am conveying what you yourself think too. You have always said, "I think those things too, but you give expression to them." Precisely. That's why I regard you as a goddess in the flesh. Nothing human is beneath you—an old Latin saying.

You make me think of the Dalai Lama. He who understands, does not preach, begs us to be happy *and* compassionate. I can feel your newborn relaxation. Bravo! You can't go wrong! You are always on the Path, and gradually becoming the Path itself, yourself.

My love embraces every part and parcel of your being and your flesh simultaneously. I know your love for me is sublime. That's all I wanted to say. Good night again.

Dream hard!

HENRY

P.S. The airmail envelope I had written out quite some days ago, when I wondered where you were. But never got round to writing the letter. Here it is at last! "Happy" Yom Kippur!

H.M.

Your birthday 11/10/78

Darling Brenda—

This is a difficult letter for me to write to you. I reread your *marvelous* letter to me and was moved to tears. *But,* I have a little bone to pick with you. In your letter you say that I never ask anything of you, that you are the one who asks.

Brenda, that disturbed me. Only a letter or two ago I wrote you a special letter, asking if you would grant me a "little" favor. (Forgive me if I call it a *little* favor.) Anyway, you ignored the plea. In a way, and you are aware of it, I am sure, ever since I know you I have been silently asking the same question. As you well surmise, it has to do with sex. Now I am not brash or foolish or dotty enough to ask you to go to bed with me. I can well imagine how repugnant it must be for a young beautiful creature like you to be asked to make love to a man almost 90 years old.

Realizing that, I have never made any direct overtures. In addition, your silent rejection of any sex business has imposed on me a self-created impotency. For a long while I thought I might be impotent. Then one day you sat beside me and told me (so wonderfully) your version of the Smith-Pocahontas affair. At first I thought what you were telling me was the result of great research on your part. But when you got to narrating how by her great love Pocahontas restored Captain John Smith's potency, I suspected that that bit was your invention. And I not only wondered about it but I thought how very wonderful of you to have thought up such an idea. (Could it be that Brenda-Pocahontas was merely proving what powers her love had?)

Anyway, and I blush to admit it, this little "invention" got me to thinking—how come Brenda, who loves me dearly, does not or will not make similar overtures with me? And then I put it out of my head as being too much to ask or even dream of.

But every time I see you the emphasis is on the sacred body. And that is quite all right, seeing as how you are blessed, like a goddess. Only there is always one aspect of the body that is ignored—and that is the sexual. Yet who better incarnates the spirit of sex than you, Brenda the Venus?

To speak of myself again for a moment. Up until I met you it did not seem possible for a man and woman to love each other deeply without the element of sex. I knew that you were not anti-sex, but just fighting off the wolves who would devour you. But I am not in that category, however sexual I may be. For me sex has always been a very natural, easy procedure. I have led a very sex-filled life. And now, in my old age, I find myself being regarded as a lovable guru *and* anchorite. I am not supposed to have a pair of balls, and the thing that goes with it.

What am I driving at? Simply this—I don't expect you to let me fuck you. (I doubt anyway that I could satisfy a sexy creature like yourself.) But I do think we ought to be on more familiar terms—that you should allow *me*—if no one else—the privilege of touching your private parts—of fondling you, in other words. And perhaps vice versa. In other words, we ought to permit ourselves to act naturally and instinctively.

If you disagree, please tell me. Just don't evade or ignore me. I will love you always, no matter what your attitude. I realize that I am taking a great risk in writing you this way, but I just have to. I am what I am, God help me. Further, it is I who am always telling people to be themselves. I don't want to be a Buddha, a St. Francis, or a St. Anthony, but just what I am—Henry Miller.

P.S. Brenda, did you take with you the photo of the two of us approaching one another to kiss but being a foot apart? I'd love to have that one, too. I look at the one you left in awe and amazement.

H.M.

P.P.S. I may enclose a few items I think will interest, delight, and disturb you too, perhaps. Forever body and soul!

•

I really didn't answer in a letter or on the phone, but the next day I went over to his house after a ballet class. I was wearing a white Grecian robe. I walked in his bedroom and said, "Henry, about that request . . ."

He was sitting in bed and I dropped the robe from my shoulders to the floor. I didn't say a word. I pulled the robe back on. He smiled, I smiled, and then I left.

•

6:15 Tuesday

Dear Brenda—

Ever there in my brain cells is the image of you lifting off your dress to show me your teats. What a moment! What commotion. And coupled with the audacity of the gesture goes that ineffable silence of yours, a silence as of antiquity, the face never contorted with passion but always calm, serene, *beatific*.

Your

HENRY

Dear, dear Brenda—

Thanksgiving is in a day or two and I doubt that I will see you over the holidays. Tomorrow comes Pamela Burke of the *Tomorrow Show*— Tom Snyder's sec'y or something to look the ground over. Val will cook a Thanksgiving dinner. I wish you could join us but you no doubt have plans of your own.

Anyway, I write not to tell you these trifles but to tell you how much you mean to me—and more and more each week. You have literally grown into my soul. You mean more to me than all the others put together. You are *all woman*. Integral. Unswerving. 100% reliable. Equal to all emergencies. Made not only for love but for everything a man's heart desires. I love you with an Orphic love. I love you from the clithonian depths, as Joyce might say. I love everything about you— your looks, your walk, the way you dress, your voice, the *beau* in your Mississippi eyes, your voice, your Southern accent (barely perceptible), your Southern background, your manners, your stance, your uniqueness. Above all, I love the way you love me. It is noble, ancient, godlike. I bless you whenever I think of you. Is it because we see so little of each other that we live such a *harmonious* romance? Harmony is rather a rare thing in my life with women. Incidentally, if Tony doesn't hide it away before you come again, ask to see a sheet of W.C. paper (written out a few years ago) which is entirely covered with the first names of women I have known more or less intimately. It's quite amazing. And somehow reflects either on my poor judgement or my bad behavior.

Brenda, I love your flesh as much as your spirit. You are that rare combination of "body and soul."

Again, my gratitude, my blessings, my prayers for you—

YOUR HENRY

1979

Sat. Eve. 11:30 P.M. 1/27/79

My treasure—

Got up to pen you a few words as you are occupying my mind like an incubus. And as I slipped out of bed, the words (in German) came back to me from *The Blue Angel*. "Ich bin von Kopf bis Fusz auf liebe eingesteldt, und das ist meine Welt und sonst garnichts." Roughly— "From head to foot I'm imbued with love, and that's my world and nothing but."

My dear one, I don't care if I can't sleep, or if I can't do this or that (chiefly *that*—just so long as you are there and thinking of me). You are my whole world—*und sonst garnichts*. In German this last sounds wonderful.

I wish I could write you in Russian, in Aztec, in Armenian, and Iranian. Because *you* are *un*limited. You are what the Greeks call "nothing in moderation." You are Mona, Anaïs, Lisa, *tout le monde*, all combined. Fire, air, earth, ocean, sky, and stars.

Your letters are out of this world. You have the knack for saying just the right thing. What you say only *you* can say. Inimitable. Superb. Seductive. Sensual. Considerate as a cherubim. Sure, you have that thing between your legs as do all women, but with you it becomes an invisible jewel, a magic touchstone, a golden Easter Egg like from the beginning of the Universe. Guard it sacredly. Worship it in private— and in public pretend it isn't there. Pretend that there you carry an opium pipe or whatever. Be the woman always but act it out like a man. Never lose faith! You are protected. Your day is dawning. Don't ask for too much—only what you can handle—and fondle.

I go back to bed now. I am at great peace loving you so much. You are my blessing. May the good Lord watch over you always!

Your

HENRY

Midnight   2/21/79

Dear One,

Can't sleep yet for thinking of you *and* St. Augustine. Here is one saying of his—"He who does not know what love is does not know who he is."

The theme of the Professor's pseudo passion play is Eros vs. Agape or in our language—Earthly love versus Heavenly love.

His play, as I told you earlier—I am now reading a revised version—makes me and Augustine close friends. Augustine approves of my rebel nature, my passion (both earthly and heavenly), my isolation, etc., etc. In fact, I am flattered by the parallelism between us. Did I ever tell you how in Paris once a poor bookdealer friend of Durrell's asked me to read Augustine's *City of God* and annotate it heavily. I did; took me about six weeks, too. But never received a cent or even an acknowledgement of my work. Until fifteen or twenty years later—said he was sorry but never made compensation or returned the book. The reason I like Augustine is because he is so human, so poor a saint, and a renegade to boot. But his talk is sublime and all based on *Love* (committed all the sins before being converted). In the play by the Professor he makes an analogy between our times and the fall of the Roman Empire (or the Civilization of the Pagan world). And my position in literature today is being likened to that of Augustine's at the fall of Rome.

Had interesting letter from Durrell, which please remind me to show you. Also a wonderful 12 page letter from Bert Mathieu. Evidently he met Blaise Cendrars' daughter Miriam while in Europe and she asked if he would help to edit and publish our correspondence. (Marvelous, as he is my "hero.") *But*, I don't remember corresponding with him at all. And she thinks it is unique, great, etc., etc.

Then my eye doctor brought me copies of a huge stack of letters to my life-long friend Emil Schnellock, which I thought lost. Someone sold them to a collector. But I could have them published. They are voluminous, weigh several pounds. I don't know if I shall start reading them.

Also a wonderful letter from an Indian who takes me for a "guru." Praises my admixture of sex and religion. In India, as I often tell you, the gods are very human—fuck their heads off. The vestal virgins are temple prostitutes. The monks and nuns cohabit. I will be getting from him two copies (for you and me) of the doctrine and methodology of Tantric Yoga (God through Sex!). Enuf. More when we meet.

HENRY

P.S. Too bad there is always a time lapse between what happens here and when I see you. Tomorrow your coming will seem like Christmas to a spiritually impoverished Christian. I love you on all fronts. I feel "corroborated" tonight, and *très* humble. *Love is all.*

HENRY

P.S. Augustine even says we have in common "our love for love," or with love.

Sunday   2/25/79

Dear Heart *(Cuore)*—

Just returned from Imperial Gardens with Bob Snyder. Kept thinking of you all evening tho' I maintained a rattling conversation throughout. Anyway, as we enter my hall I say to Bob, "Who wrote that poem, you know, it has a line in it like this—'I have been faithful to thee, O Cynara, after my fashion.' (And suddenly I remembered the name of the poet—Ernest Dowson, an Englishman.)

And so I too have been faithful in my fashion to my dear, dear Brenda, the star of my life, the light of my soul, the buttress against all misfortune. I hope you are well and snoring as I pen these hasty lines.

An actress in the booth next to ours was giving me the eye all evening. When she got up to go she stopped to shake hands and ask who I was. I said, "Another human being like yourself." "He who does not know love does not know who he is." I know love and you and who I am.

LUCKY HENRY

3/6/79

Dear Heart—

Having a double photo of you around keeps you not only in heart but in mind and soul. I live with you here as if we were united in marriage. Thank God it's a heavenly marriage and not an earthly one. More and more I sense the spiritual, ordained nature of our relationship. You are the goddess Isis unveiled.

The notes accumulating in my mind for our "Scenario" tend to be shocking, revealing the duality of all my experiences. With you it is a real, true union, even if missing in the flesh. Even were you to fuck your head off, as we say, you would remain "inviolate." You are the magnificent one, the *ne plus ultra* of womanhood.

> Bless you, love you,
> adore you.
>
> HENRY   (MIDNIGHT)

P.S. Almost had sunstroke today!!

SCENARIO

Early Remembrances:

1) Born with a silver spoon in my mouth. Got everything I craved, except a real pony. Writing Santa to send me a drum *and* a magic lantern. Returning work socks and mittens to teacher in kindergarten— to give to the poor in the class. When my mother sees me returning from kindergarten Christmas Eve and no gifts she asks what happened. I say, "Nothing, I just returned them to the teacher. I know Santa is going to bring me better things." With this she slaps me hard, grabs the lobe of one ear, and drags me one long block to the school, to apologize to the teacher for my rudeness.

I couldn't understand what I had done wrong . . . this was our first big misunderstanding. It registered deeply (I never forgot nor forgave) and left in my childish mind the feeling that my mother was stupid and cruel.

In later years I only slightly modified this view of my mother. She always pretended to be proud of me but she neither understood nor loved me.

Next to kindergarten episode, around same period, is when she shows me a wart on her finger which is annoying her and I say, "Why don't you cut it off?" And she does, gets blood poisoning, and a few days later, when I am sitting in my little chair by the fire, she comes over to me, scowling and threatening (her finger now heavily bandaged), and slaps me some more, saying, "You were the one who told me to cut the wart off!"

As she lies abed, only a few days away from death, I bring my friend Vincent to see her. He is handsome, well-mannered, and an air pilot.

My mother's eyes glow when she sees him. It is obvious that she has immediately taken him to heart. Suddenly, she raises herself from the pillow—I am standing by the side of the bed—and exclaims, "If only I had a son like you, Vincent," looking me in the eye while speaking. (And I was fresh from Europe where I was idolized as a great American writer. All this meant nothing to her. She never forgave me for becoming a writer instead of a tailor!)

The culminating and rather gruesome final episode takes place in a funeral parlor where she is laid out in state for her friends and relatives to say farewell to her. She is there about a week before being buried. I visit the place now and then—not every day. Each time I come and bend over the coffin one of her eyes opens, as if to stare at me. It seems to me she is *reproving* me even in death. It gives me shivers. I always notify the director of the funeral parlor who always closes the eye without saying a word.

Thursday—10:00 P.M.   3/15/79

My darling Brenda—

I am so filled with you I am spilling over. Thinking of you continually and praying for your hopes, wishes, dreams to come through.

For *me* you are already *through*—thru the net of obstacles, I mean.

You are one of the famous Greek goddesses—there were quite a few, you know. Women weren't always the pawns of men. And some were wild and fierce.

I have had a week with Bert Mathieu, a truly illumined mind. Absorbed more knowledge from him and some psychic sustenance from his adored "Geri." I had thought, from what he had written me about her, that I would be out-countenanced—but it turned out the other way round.

Brenda, must I say it for the 1000th time—yes, I must . . . *I love you!!!* So simple, yet means all the world to me . . . Now I can go to bed and to sleep. I will be right beside you, holding you tight and lovingly. *Tenderly.* I have two prefaces to write; one for the French about *Journal of Albion Moonlight* and one for my own unfinished book on D. H. Lawrence, which Noel Young will bring out next year. I will make special references to Lawrence's *The Apocalypse* (to my mind his best work), not to *Women in Love* or *Aaron's Rod*. Excuse me once again for derailing.

I am getting to be a genuine "solipsist"—and this is not a "sole-cism." (Two 50 cent words!)

Dear, dear Brenda—sleep well. Lose all your aches and pains, wake up lively and healthy. Remain as always—"indomitable," yet tender, loving, giving. God is with you and all the little "gods" who ran the ancient world.

You are a modern "Semiramis."

Bless you, love you to death. Take your time answering. I can bide my time—so long as I know you love me—*and you do*, that I am sure of.

Yours now, hereafter and in between.

HENRY THE
INAMORATA!

Friday 3/23/79

My lovely, only one!

What a beautiful night it was last night! I went to bed so happy—hope you did too.

I am enclosing a thing I wrote on Kenneth Patchen some years ago. Got it from my Bibliographer—for use in a French book on Patchen.

I send it along because it seems to reaffirm many of the thoughts I was elaborating on last night at dinner. (Incidentally, you are about the first Southern woman I have known who was not also a great talker. I mean—too much talky-talk. Your talk comes out of a serene silence.) Hells bells, you are not just a Mississippi gal, you're part Navajo, I learn to my heart's content last night. Your Indian blood accounts for your persistence and resistance, for your determination with which you are blessed, and also for your "nobility of character," I honestly believe. You have more virtues than one can shake out of a hat.

Was at dentist today. Almost false alarm. A mere trifle, an adjustment. Hope I get good news tomorrow from my oculist. And you, are you just fine and dandy today? (I trust Charals will be satisfied with the water color. If he wants another, I'll give him one. Like that he'd get his four thousand.) I am going to experiment with some weak ones I did by going over them with ink drawings—against the grain, so to speak. By that I mean the drawing will bear no relation to the already "finished" water color. Follow me? This is always a good method. One thing over against another—instead of "blending."

I have written a dozen or more letters thus far. This is my last for today.

You know what? I can see you *and* me in the photo just a little better each morning. If I saw *you* every day, in the flesh, I probably wouldn't need to use glasses. (I'd use a microscope!) Signing off now— happy days. Love you to death. Love you awake and asleep. Forever!

HENRY

DREAM OF 3/25/79

As in similar scenes heretofore what occurs here takes place in public view, though not intentionally. As in that erotic Japanese film, *The Realm of the Senses, you* take the lead.

Somehow we are in the lobby of a grand hotel when the desire comes over you. You say to me, "Let's do it here!" Impulsively, just like that. I seem taken aback, more aware perhaps of where we are in space and time. Not too much so, though always in these intimate encounters there are only you and me in the world—no matter if people are floating about us. I suppose this represents our great passion for one another—we can shut the world out.

Anyway, in the twinkle of an eye, you have made us gravitate toward a conspicuous and royal-looking couch in the very center of the lobby. Before I can utter a word of protest, you have unzipped fly and are holding my penis in your hand. I have full erection—it feels marvelous. With the same swiftness you lift your dress, exposing yourself completely and with that we tumble onto the couch. As I am about to enter you I remember that only recently you have had the copper coil removed. (I wonder to myself if you know what you are doing or if, like after that proverbial drink of champagne, you are powerless to do otherwise.)

Entering you is so smooth and easy it is almost unreal. I try to look you in the face, to note your expression. But, just as when lying in my own bed and regarding our photo without benefit of glasses, there are only pale outlines of your visage to be seen. At any rate, I am at once convinced that you want it this way, that you are conscious of what you are doing. And this only heightens the ecstasy which has gripped us. I cannot help but think of all the negative reactions you have manifested and now this complete, utter surrender. You are squirming like an eel, whispering softly in my ear, "Do it, do it, Henry!" and I do it to the best of my ability, more impressed by your willingness than by my unexpected prowess. Your cunt, incidentally, is all I had ever imagined it to be. It is an "answering" cunt, if you know what I mean.

In the very midst of our secret enjoyment, I feel a rough tug on the shoulder and a harsh voice shouting, "What the hell do you think you're doing here? Where do you think you're at?" And with this he yanks me to my feet, my penis hanging out of my fly, and a few drops of sperm falling onto the plush.

He then addresses you. You have already pulled down your skirt. But you have a crestfallen look on your face. "Young lady," he begins, "I wonder if you know what you are up to or where you are . . ."

You interrupt by saying, "I'm terribly sorry, Sir, but I completely forgot where I was or what I was doing."

"You did, did you?" says the manager. "What *are* you anyway—*an actress?*"

"Exactly!" You reply. "You see I have a bad habit of forgetting my lines at times. Just now I was enacting an imaginary scene from *Wuthering Heights.*"

Now the little crowd which has gathered about us begins to titter. A few applaud. One shouts, "Bravo!"

With this you seem to regain your composure. You take my arm with your two hands and escort us both to the door. Under your breath you say to me, "Fuck those idiots! They wouldn't recognize a good piece of acting if it were shoved under their nose." You give me a little hug and add, "Come Henry, let's go somewhere and have a quiet drink together. You were superb, do you know that?"

FINIS

4/17/79

My dear, dear Brenda—

A short one at the end of a hectic day to tell you how much I adore you and also that I am more than ever confident I shall bring you good fortune—and soon. I feel, oddly enough, that the Creator has given me extra powers (such as luck, happiness, and other things) to bestow on others.

You are always uppermost in my mind. I love you more than ever.

You are all in all to me, ever. I venerate your name, revere your body and soul. You are giving me an added lease on life. Let us shine out and win out together!

Your beloved

HENRY

P.S. The moon has been full for several days it seems. A *good* augur!

April 30, 1979

Dearest, most beloved Brenda—

I found your letter in the mail box shortly after it was dropped in— *by you?* And here I am again, relieving myself, as it were. Let's call what follows—"The Revolt of the Animal." Anatole France (19th century writer) wrote a marvelous book called *Revolt of the Angels.*

Angels is the clue. Your letter was written to a mythical demi-god. Perhaps by now you have received the three letters which reveal the god's feet of clay. Certainly I appreciate and am thrilled by all the wonderful encomiums you bestow on me, *but* . . . where is H.M. the human being, the male, the hungry lover?

You know, if we are to believe the Christians, even God Almighty had to send a son who was human, all too human. Even God must get lonely in his High Heaven.

I hope you have forgiven my rather crude outburst—last letter—but the animal in me just could hold back no longer. He doesn't want to be loved solely as an unusual human being, but he wants both sides of the coin to be recognized. Indeed, without that "base" side of the coin he would not be what he is. I say "base," but I don't mean it. It's not *base,* it's merely the very human, very animalistic side of one's being. Just as God-given as the brain or the soul.

When I saw you again in *FM* I fell apart. Even in the old days of burlesque, they never presented such an erotic picture as you gave in that scene. (Though frankly I never understood a word of what either of you said!) It seemed to me that you were doing your best to seduce him. (Am I all wrong again?)

You looked absolutely ravishing. Like one who not only wished to ravage but *also-to-be-ravished*! When you semi-reclined with feet facing him it was like murmuring, "Fuck me, please. I'm dying for it!"

What acting! Ultra realistic! Sensual but divinely so, as if you were one of those Hindu goddesses come to earth for a quick lay. Even walking along the street it was erotic. Just in a brassiere—a low-slung one too, which gave a good view of your inimitable teats. Every inch of you was on fire, it seemed. Reminded me of that first letter you wrote wherein you said you were just one big "erogenous" creature. What a starter that was!

And now we embrace like brother and sister—perhaps a trifle incestuously, but still brother-sister. As I have said several times, why can't you to permit me to caress you, touch you anywhere and everywhere, except in our dreams? What have you to fear or lose? Do you imagine that I will lose all respect for you? Impossible!

Forgive this long tirade. You know it is Love talking, not just crude desire. I want all your love, not just admiration and adulation.

I must stop—my back aches horribly.

Henry

May 1st, 1979

Darling Brenda—

I thought it was midnight but clock says only 10:20 P.M. So I have time to pen a few more lines.

How good it was to receive your call! Your voice is so soothing, so "convincing." Strange word, eh—*convincing*? But I mean that if I had entertained the slightest doubts about you, your voice would immediately dispel them. You sound so honest, so thoroughly genuine, it's just amazing. I suppose that all my life, through my many marriages, I had met with so many lies, such deceit, that to come upon someone like yourself who is all gold is almost unbelievable.

A strange corollary between you and the woman in this book about the Turkish harem. She *never* unveils her face. He has not even caught a glimpse of her eyes. Yet here is this strong, vital affinity between them, despite differences in race, age, customs, etc. And you are the "Untouchable" one. But the attraction is there, just as strong, *chez vous* as *chez moi*, I feel. After our talk on phone I must apologize for imputing to you feelings you did not possess. You tell me you *acted out* this seductive scene on T.V. And I believe you wholeheartedly. But God, what must you be like when it is *real*? Like that sirocco wind from the desert, no doubt, that withers and melt all it contacts.

Reading *Disenchanted* makes me realize how lucky, how very lucky I am to have *you*. Instead of "disenchanted" I am under a perpetual spell of enchantment. Like Tristan (of the opera), someone must have slipped me a drug in my sleep. I am all love, all devotion, completely obsessed. Bless you for it. It is often agonizing but also bliss. A sweet mixture—like "the sweet waters of Asia." Now I can return to bed in peace. I am with you heart and soul. Nothing to ask for, nothing to seek. You are you and I am I. And we have met and are conjoined in some sacred fashion.

HENRY

Friday   May 11, 1979

Dearest, most beloved Brenda—

Your letter this noon created a bit of havoc in me. I am sorry to say so but both your physical condition, your psychological attitude, *and* your philosophy of life—all rub me the wrong way. You are taking life too cavalierly, too much bravado, if I may say so. One has to be more humble. You were not put here just to make a big splash, and then vanish. Who do you think you are? Alexander the Great conquered the world before he was 30, but died alone in the heart of India, enjoying nothing from his extraordinary endeavors. We are here to enjoy life, to make the most of it, not to create a sensation and a big name.

You can't do everything at once. Why should you? You are not really enjoying life—you are just exercising your way through it. Hercules wasn't the greatest of the gods, though he may have been the strongest. (Don't confuse health with strength.) No, your recklessness reminds me of battle scenes in the War Between the States. The "rebels" (you all) were admired even by the Yankees for their intrepid dash and verve, for their *recklessness*. You are IT.

Brenda, I don't want you to go before me. Nor do I like to think I am just your crutch. My thought is to be together (for pleasure, enjoyment, growth) just as long as possible. I can't picture myself burying you. (Besides, your mother would never forgive me. Where was I, a grown man, when her beautiful daughter was killing herself with work? And so on and so forth.) And she would be right. You tell me always how much I teach you, but if I haven't taught you how to live I haven't taught you anything. *To live*—that is the primary thing. Live in every root branch of your being! Get me?

Brenda, dear Brenda, love means more than just being a shining star for the other person. If I thought you were killing yourself just to prove something to the world, or your parents, or me, I would urge you to desist. You don't have to prove anything to anyone. (In short, "don't look for miracles, *you* are the miracle.") And, as the good St. Francis said—this is *for me*!!—"Don't try to change the world. Change worlds." You see, in one sense you weren't so far off the track when you started out to be a nun. There was beauty and purity and significance in that narrow little world. This big, noisy outer world is just full of shit. There are no real values. It wouldn't matter what you elected to be so long as you remained strictly yourself and kept an eye on the eternal values.

I think I've said about all I meant to. I hope you know it was done with *love*. Yes, I love *you* more than life, but it's life that keeps us loving, no? It was so good to get that surprise call this A.M. Means everything to me. Do pay heed now.

HENRY

P.S. I know it's impossible for you to make a great change in your life. Few of us ever do or can. But you could try a little moderation and a little more joy of life—not all work and exercise!

Friday 5:00 P.M.

Beloved!

I think of you running around in spite of your cold. What a brave woman you are!

What I can never understand, or swallow, is how despite all your activities, everything comes about so slowly. Is it the angel in you that gets in the way, I wonder. You should be taken "on sight."

I had to laugh (to myself) when you referred to Warren Beatty as a "gentleman." You mean, of course, a *Southern* gentleman. Just as I always make a distinction between a *British* gentleman and a real gentleman. The real gentleman is capable of making a *faux pas* but it is immediately overlooked.

I have to stop here because my sight is so bad. I love you so much and feel so helpless now when you need help and attention. It makes me feel sad.

Keep wrapped up warm when you go out, dear Brenda. Don't let yourself get chilled. If there's anything I can do for you let me know. Now back to bed again. I love you dearly, dearly.

HENRY

Sunday Night

Dearest Brenda—

After phoning you and hearing of your Indian grandmother it occurred to me to suggest that when you have good talk some night mention absence of copper coil and see if Indians had their own form of protection, probably without use of any mechanical whatnot or drug. They probably used herbs in one form or another.

Funny thought, eh? But I have a great respect for Indian knowledge. D. H. Lawrence speaks in one of his books of seeing an Indian in afternoon with badly sprained ankle. That evening he saw the man dance, leg looked perfectly normal. Have their own healing arts—all primitive peoples do.

I love you so much, so tenderly. All day yesterday had you on my mind incessantly. You know, for all the "randy" letters I write you, when awake and thinking of you I never think those thoughts. Oh, yes, I'd like to touch—but that's all. You're too beautiful and holy to be desecrated. Imagine this from the author of *Tropic of Cancer*! Ho Hum! Tee hee!

HENRY

P.S. I must repeat—I love you profoundly. If New Mexico will regenerate you, go. And with you will go all my prayers and wishes. You may have to miss seeing Beatty (June 20th), but we can always get him another time!

11:30 P.M.   July 7, 1979

Darling Brenda—

It's just a half hour since you phoned me to tell me how happy you were this day. How happy that made me you will never know.

After you phoned I thought of another curious parallelism in our lives. Where Englund told you it was not easy to place you—you were not typical—the same thing happened several times to me when I was struggling with editors and publishers. The editor who paid me $350.00 (In 1920's—worth $1200 then) for my article on *Words* told me they couldn't publish it in their mag because it was "too good." And you may recall how the famous editor of the Dictionary wrote my father a letter after I had interviewed him, saying, "Your son is a genius." And my old man looking at me blankly and saying, "Does he mean *you?*"

Yes, Brenda, you will burst like a rocket when you get that first good part. Instant recognition. People already recognize you for what you are. I kiss you now just on the brow, as one would the statue of Venus de Milo or an Indian (Hindu) goddess. Blessings on you and more joy, more good luck!

Good night dear heart!

Henry

Monday—11:00 P.M.

Darling—

Just got up to go to kitchen and see what time it is. Wondering if you are sweating your ass off doing that scene in class.

Brenda dear, funny I should have to tell you, a Mississippi girl, how to behave in a terrible heat wave like this. You've got to get quiet *inside*, not complain or combat it, but play dead dog. Just do nothing but lie in bed or on floor. Give yourself up to erotic fantasies. The heat stirs your blood, makes you horny, swells your genitals, gives you a perpetual yearn for intercourse. Play with yourself if necessary, but don't try to cool off when there ain't no coolin' off. One has to just grin and bear it.

I hope it cools off enuf by Thursday so that we can go to the Gardens. If it's too bloody hot we ought to just stay home, you in your smoke house and me in mine. But I'm dying to see you. Hoping I may even see you before Thursday just to touch you in a gorgeous flimsy dress. Don't wear pants these days. Keep the air circulating between your legs. Imagine you are giving in to your feelings.

Signing off now because I want to dream of you for the next nine hours at least . . . How did the rehearsal turn out Saturday night? That scene should have been a complete farce.

Take good care in this heat. Nothing strenuous. Just float with the tide. If you sweat, all the better.

Your incurable romantic and everlasting lover,

HENRY

Tuesday   July 18, 1979

About *Vampirella*

I have been reading it here and there, in snatches. It sure is of our age—crazy, very derivative, and meant for ten year olds. But I am sticking to it. Just can't picture you reading this crap. Crap or not, in the hands of excellent men it could be made into a best seller film, I do believe. There are some amazing speeches and incidents. But in the end (to my way of thinking), it comes to "Sarsparilla," as I misunderstood you. We live in a synthetic age—the films reflect this. So even shoddy stuff finds appreciation with the mob. That *you* really liked this stuff—and still do—dumbfounds me. Leaves me "discombobulated." Do I know you? From what planet did you arrive? Who gave birth to you? How did "they" pick Mississippi? In the "gloaming"? (You rose up out of the pool gleaming like Venus Andromeda by the great Florentine painter—you know his name.)

With it all I am crazier than ever about you. My back feels broken. But my hand still holds the pen.

Long enuf to declare my undying love for you, you sweet bird of Paradise. Give my warm greetings to your Navajo grandmother. Write a little note to me when or if you ever find the time.

Your everlasting love

HENRY

August 20, 1979

Yes, my *dear, dear Brenda*, when I miss you, long for you, wonder where you are, even *I* "know what sorrow is." But usually I am spared that emotion. You keep me informed of your whereabouts, you call me at all hours of day or night, bless your soul.

I feel you are never "away" from me. I have no womb to carry you in, nor that sack the Australian kangaroo carries things in, but my heart and soul, my very guts carry you constantly.

Oh Brenda, it's so obvious to me that all the world loves you, adores you. Don't ever let anyone get you down. Remember always who you are—the Queen. You were born one and you will die one. You are better than Corelli, Anaïs, June—the whole shebang. You were made to be admired by geniuses only, who are true appreciators. Must quit. Back aches and buttocks. That's love ain't it?

I give you all kinds of love, unadulterated. All from the heart.

HENRY

P.S. If I were a real artist I would add a few sketches of you or imaginary portraits. I hate to sign off still full up with you. Even my balls ache for you! There!

August 28, 1979

Dearest Brenda, my love, my life!

That *I* could have hurt you—shown such disrespect, as you put it, stupefies me. If I am guilty, I apologize with all my heart.

Brenda, you ask about permission to do the two films. Of course. Only I wonder if it's wise to ask my publisher for the rights to *both* at once. They may wonder if you represent a corporation. If and when you do write, write to Griselda Ohanessian (Armenian, I believe) although she is not in charge of "Permissions." But she likes and understands me and will take care of you. You spoke of knowing millionaires from whom it would not be difficult to raise four million dollars. That almost took my breath away because I always thought millionaires were the hardest to extract money from. I was turned down by a millionaire for $100 loan—and I was then famous. All my aid has come from the poor in hand but rich in heart.

Dear, dearest Brenda, light of my life. I do hope to live on (selfishly) just to have your love.

Forever and ever

YOURS!

P.S. What must the sinner do to redeem himself?

Columbus Day—Monday

Chérie—

Do I dare write in this sort of handwriting on that ink drawing you think worthy of a birthday gift the following? (The first few words are from a poem by Baudelaire.)

> Il sera au-delà comme ici-bas;
> soleil, étoiles, montagnes, oiseaux, fleurs,
> pédérastes et les amours sublimes, comme c'est le cas
> pour moi et toi.

Translated: *It will be the same in the beyond as here below;* Sun, stars, mountains, birds, flowers, pederasts, and sublime loves, as is the case with you and me.

(The underlined words are Baudelaire's. The rest is mine.)
Tout pour aujourd'hui.

"Le bel aujourd'hui!"

HENRY

Written in flowing style, *comme ceci*—

●

Henry had a recurring dream, which he was unable to figure out to his satisfaction. One night he called around 2:00 A.M. and told me that I was the curly-haired little girl who stood by his side to protect him like a ministering angel. I don't recall his talking about the dream again.

●

Thanksgiving, 1979

Dear Brenda,

A dream I had again last night. Lots of people gathered but the one who sticks close is a little curly-headed girl about 6 or 7 years of age. Cute, sensitive, never leaves side of my bed. Then there is a giantess who looks like a Matisse portrait. She is about 8 feet tall and wears a floppy, straw hat—huge which adds to her grotesque figure. There are a few women only about 4 feet tall, with hair twisted into little knots, top of head. Some *quite* ugly. No beautiful voices—just a steady drone. When this vision of things vanishes—suddenly as it comes—I hear voices and music—mostly from popular music turn of the century 1900—like "Wait till the Sun Shines Nelly," "School Days," "Meet Me Tonight in Dreamland, Roses, roses, roses, keep dreaming of you dear," and then a steady hum or murmur of voices speaking unintelligibly. I wonder at times if it is a prelude to going nuts.

I wonder how you are doing back home. How is Sally Venus and is Joey not there? (Let's not speak of the Devil!) But I'm sure he'll be eatin' his turkey Thanksgiving. (Just now, when I turned my head, the curly-haired girl was at my side looking up at me. Kinda cute, as I saw. I guess my eyes are tired out. But every day there's a slew of mail.)

HM

12:30 P.M.   Tuesday night

Brenda, Brenda—

I can't sleep for thinking of you. Have been walking around the joint aimlessly—for mere exercise, so to speak.

What bothers me is—well, a number of things. How you will manage all alone in Paris. Or, if you take on a gallant troubador, how you will keep him out of your boudoir. The French are anything but romantic. Like Shylock, they demand their pound of flesh.

In my head I go through so many imaginary conversations which you carry on with the cavaliers who will pursue you. (Will put them in French Notebook for you!)

Your French teacher ought to be teaching you how to manage when in Paris—idiomatic expressions. Not just "Écoute!" You need some rudimentary grammar: Tenses, conjugations, genders, *la politesse*, etc.

Now I recall where Hotel Le Royal is: on Blvd. Raspail just a few doors past intersection with Blvd. du Montparnasse.

Keep wondering who could be your guide and protector—take you to modest hotels and restaurants, etc., etc. (How to pronounce "Monsieur.")

It burns me up that I can't accompany you. Also, what you should answer when fans question you about me. I don't think they know how physically disabled I am. And why and how you should have me in this condition.

Brenda, dear Brenda, I trust you implicitly. I just want to make it smoother sailing for you. Ask your French girl friends about hotel rates—modest hotels—and modest restaurants—where they are.

Everything has changed tremendously since I was there last. For instance, *le pourboire* (tip) for madame in charge of *les cabinets* (toilets & phone) used to be 10 or 15 centimes. Today they are thinking to abolish the centime, just as we think to do away with pennies.

There's so much to know in advance. You won't be able to float around as you did when last there. *And,* be careful about jogging. Traffic in Paris is murderous. They don't stop to let pedestrians cross—they run you down.

I remember now one of my favorite modest restaurants: Res. des Sts.-Pères corner rue des Sts.-Pères and Boulevard St.-Germain. I remember famous hotel Oscar Wilde slept in—near l'Académie des Beaux Arts, rue Bonaparte.

Lots of things are returning to mind. All I want is your safety and comfort.

Made two water colors today. One quite good, I think. The other by a "lunatic," largely *crayon* or water color tubes. Hope you'll be well by Thursday, don't push things. Give your body a chance to recover from the tough regimen you live by! *All my devout love!*

HENRY

Wednesday

Dear Heart—

Brr—but it's cold this a way! Enuf to freeze the nuts off a brass monkey. Last night Maureen cooked dinner and today she dropped in the mail box a list of Paris (good, modest) hotels ranging from $30 to $50 a night. Doesn't sound too bad! Hope you're still hitching up with Kristine Hurrell.

Sava and I spent 2½ hours Saturday night doping out a letter to Fellini in French. When finished I was too tired to tackle one for François Truffaut. Maybe you might write him in English, just as you feel. In that way you might hit the right note! (Imagine if I had had such a letter from you in the beginning? *Or did I?* I seem to remember photos more than anything. Those wonderful teats, slim waist, stunning legs.

What a beauty!) Can still picture you, as you first appeared to me. You haven't changed. You grow more ethereal, more magnetic, more close to perihelion all the time.

I must stop now, my darling. My eye begins to feel the strain. More later—don't worry.

Maybe I'll call early in the A.M.

> Yours for Eternity my beloved!
>
> HENRY

11/14/79

Brenda, Brenda, how to tell you all you mean to me, both in spirit and in the flesh. Sometimes I think I am like one of the Christian saints—overflowing with desire! At other moments just satisfied to worship you from afar, knowing I have your love and complete understanding. Always picturing you in my mind in Paris or New Orleans—some rambunctious place where vestal virgins do not go, but where every other critter has an erection or a body full of lust. (And I am far away— see nothing, say nothing, hear nothing, *know nothing*. Dreading to hear the word *champagne*. Hoping you will have a companion, like Christine Hurrell, who knows her way around and speaks the language.)

Est-ce que tu me suis? (Follow me?) What lessons I have yet to give you. And what embraces! Will never get enough of you, never love you enuf, never have enough of you. You are with me always, always and forever. You are the *crème de la crème, le ne plus ultra, la bien aimée. Tout, tout.* I hope you are reciprocating *mentally.* Tomorrow (or tonight) the Imperial Gardens. If only I were forty years younger. You deserve it. But I love you with all that's in me—*toujours et à Jamais!*

I go to bed now to dream of you. Thank God it's class night, not "frivolity" night.

> Bless you, my beloved!
>
> May you be forever in God's hands!
>
> HENRY

What more can one give than *Love?*

Sunday 6:30 P.M.

Dear, loving Brenda—

How like a ministering angel you were today. So patient, so attentive, so *serviable*. And you showed no chagrin when Dr. Sewel failed to arrive. Wonderful of you. Strangely enough, you not only have a fiery temperament but the opposite too—that is, calm, self-controlled, patient, understanding. Madame Langmann senses all these qualities in you and adores you in recognition of these and all your other virtues.

I wish I could start translating her letter now but my eyes are still sore. Now I understand why my oculist could not do more for my sight. It's this general body condition which is affecting my vision as well.

Right at my elbow lies Jacqueline's wonderful letter—and I can give only a feeble echo of it. Hardly that. Except I would have been proud had it been addressed to me. Oddly enuf it *was* addressed to *me*, but intended for you. But she's got us on the same wavelength, twin hearts and minds—and souls.

Notice too how love, when it's true and deep, is never-ending, but ripening all the time. What is so wonderful about our love is that it is constant—no quarrels and making up—no separations and reuniting, but blossoming, blossoming. Like the "Roses of Picardy," eh what?

And in such two strange beings—you from Mississippi and me from the 14th Ward, Brooklyn. Complete opposites yet one in heart and being. Vive Vivekananda!

Yes, Brenda, impulsive though you be at times, you are at bottom quite stable, always true to yourself. Jacqueline underlines your need for encouragement. But do you know what I think? That *everyone* entering this film world needs the biggest encouragement, or, to put it another way, whoever has talent (or genius) has a tough time of it in this world. This planet was not created for the likes of genius.

Add to it all, nearly everyone I know is feeling a bit discomfited, discombobulated right now. It's Uranus that's the cause of much of it, affects genius and dullard, equally. We're getting a foretaste of what's to come around 1984, I do believe. On the verge of war, disaster, etc., but shying away from it. Nobody willing to press the button for the big *shebang*. I like the French word for it—la grande *foutaise* (fuck up).

Well, dear, Bill has just walked in and is fixing some soup and more yogurt. The soup—ask your Jewish doctor—does he believe in matzoh ball chicken soup! I love the matzoh balls. But they are full of starch, *non*?

Is your French improving? Ever use it with Kristine? Good way to get real practice. Also try to read my little French book—*Je ne fouis pas plus con qui un autre.* Don't consult dictionary. Underline words or phrases you can't understand. Go back again and again—seek the *context.*

Must stop here. Do I love you? Do the stars shine? Does the earth revolve? *Where you are I am.*

YOUR BELOVED

(From Jacqueline Langmann)

Dear Henry—

. . . As for Brenda, I embrace with tenderness and I am happy to know her and never separate you both in my thoughts. I looked at your respective horoscopes, and without repeating what I already said to you both on the subject, there is profound agreement between your mutual planets. It's cut and dried . . .

In Pluto—which represents many things in life, but in particular the influence one may have over the masses, over the general public, one can find the sign of Balance, in the fifth house—love, sights and theatre—when this is in total harmony with Uranus—particularly from November 1980. It is therefore excellent for her work. Brenda has unquestionable creative gifts. I do not know how this manifests itself in her career but it is something to be encouraged.

Neptune collides with Uranus, from December 1979 up until February 1980 . . . Neptune is the illusion, therefore it is necessary to distrust it, she can be pleasant at certain moments and even encouraging but here be advised that one should have both feet on the ground. One must always guard one's health if there are small problems . . .

My letter will arrive for Xmas or for the 26th—I hope.

JACQUELINE LANGMANN

Thurs. *Late*

My dear One—

You have just left. It's as if the City had just lost all its electric power. You're gone. No see Brenda for days. Must learn to live without

Brenda. I can think; I can wait; I can do without—everything except Brenda. You are burnt into my flesh, my spirit, my all. You are so like the Navajos I read of in my youth. Appear silently, leave noiselessly—with one constantly.

Alone with my dreams . . . I no longer talk of my desires, my appetites. Too gross. You said it tonight—"delicate and elegant." Not the least bit frumptious. Always anticipating. Always on the prowl. A panther dressed in silks and ermine. A mute sleuth. A determined survivalist. Not a born again Christian but an eternal angel of goodness, mercy and light.

I bid you good night, dear heart. Dream of your coming fame and fortune!

> Your
>
> HENRY

12/29/79

Dear, dear, dearest Brenda—

I can't wait to receive your address in Paris. My heart is bursting with love and adoration. I must write you. First off, to my great surprise, I had a wonderful birthday—telegrams, phone calls from abroad, flowers galore, *and* a wonderful dinner with Barbara, Ruth, and Bill. I didn't black out as I usually do now either at breakfast or dinner. I leave the table when I feel the fade out commencing. I am still receiving congratulations. Today I had a letter from Fred or Alf or Joey. He never received a copy of the book. So he went out and bought a few and wrote me about it—a beautiful letter. Durrell also wrote me but it was largely about his new book and what he has tried to do in it—much of it over my head. He wrote me from Sommières where his eldest daughter (the actress) was visiting him.

A 9-minute selection from our radio talk went out to 200 stations. Reminds me of what Madame Langmann said about you—how you will suddenly burst upon the attention of the world. *Suddenly.*(Uranus behind it.) Oh, such good things she predicted for you. And she really loves you, as does everyone who knows you.

And only now am I coming to my love ditty about you. I got up out of bed feeling wrapped in your warmth. Yes, as if emerging from your womb. I suckled at your breast. I stared unblinkingly into your eyes. I simply gave myself to you, every parcel, every inch of loving flesh. I know you, Brenda Venus, as mother, sister, lover, goddess whom I worship. I know you and adore you in all your ways, your quirks, your imperious demands, your extraordinary gift of yourself.

Whenever I look at the clock I quickly calculate the time it is in Paris—and wonder where you are, what you are doing. Incidentally, I wonder if you weren't somewhat disappointed with Notre Dame. Chartres as a cathedral is far superior. Ask your friend. I am still trying to recall name of my favorite street. I can tell you names of where it begins and ends, if that will help. It begins at the Place de la Contrescarpe and runs like a snake down to les Gobelins. At the Place you would notice it right away—it's narrow and each side of street is crammed with food shops, the wares piled up outside on the street. Oh, what I would give to wander down that street with you. You remember *Père Goriot* by Balzac? Well, one of the several streets leading into my street was where Balzac had Père Goriot living. Another street was where the character in *Confession de Minuit* lived—another favorite French book of mine. It begins like this: "Je me nomine Louis Salavain." There is a whole series about him.

Dear Brenda—I must stop here—my eye is giving out. How tragic to be giving out on all fronts when I love you like an inspired demon (of mercy). So long for a while. No 12 page letter yet—but I have faith it will arrive. Maybe you forgot to put stamps on.

> Your most loving, most devoted
>
> HENRY

Paris   December 30, 1979

Darling Henry,

Today is Sunday Dec. 30, almost the last day of '79 and I've been in Paris over a week now. I write this to remind myself that I have only one more week and will be time to come home. I have had already the most wonderful experiences to always remember. Time flies by when one is happy and I am perpetually bedazzled (as you say). My French is starting to return, and I am beginning to feel very much at home. I feel these people like me very much and of course I am in love with every moment, every second. I cannot sleep! It has been days since I have had more than three hours per night. I go to bed early, but I keep checking the window for the daylight to creep in. Even the rain is romantic. I can't eat. I've lost pounds, not gained as you said I would. The food, of course, is excellent, but last night I went to see Nureyev's newly choreographed ballet *Manfred* and I cried, sweated, laughed and yelled "bravo" to the top of my lungs at least thirty-five times. My hands were red and burning from clapping so much. The critics slashed it to bits, but last night's crowd knew genius when they saw it, and we all went wild for this extravagant and disorderly stream of unconscious beauty, or shall I say conscious? He was superb, attentive, concentrated to the extreme of pulling me on stage to participate as a prima ballerina. After, I went to Maxim's for dinner and although the food was to die for, I could only eat a few bites . . . I was just floating on the sheer energy of Paris. I love Paris any time at all. I wish you were here to show me *your* Paris, but I carry my Little Book that you wrote for me around all over and try to see it through your eyes. I am so very glad to have my little book. It comes in quite handy.

I saw the Salvador Dali exhibit at the Pompidou Center and became a greater fan of the man. His work is so—sensual, it really did strike a number of moods in me.

Today I am off to see the Picasso exhibit. Can't wait! My feet ache from all the walking. They will never be the same, I know. I'll never be able to do ballet again.

Saw two films in French. I, actually, could understand Yves Montand. He is wonderful. Will call Lawrence Durrell today and try to go to his place. I read *Justine* and loved it. Started *Balthazar*. What a beautiful poet this man is. I hope you can feel my excitement. I do so want to share it all with you. Met your agents, Hoffman. They were very nice, very young, and not aggressive as I believe agents should be. They said we'll try to get you interviews with Truffaut and Wertmuller. I said, "It is nice that you try, but *it would be even better if you got me the meeting as Smile at the Foot of the Ladder* is one of my main reasons for coming to Paris and I do so want to make this film for Henry. I owe him so very much that I would like to present him with a sort of present." They understood. Also, our photos are hanging up in their office. Really lovely, my precious one.

Hope you are well, and in good spirits. Know I miss you, love you with all my heart, think of you constantly and will be home sooner than you can bat your beautiful blue eyes that sparkle like the stars in the sky.

I'm off to mass. I love going to church in Paris and Rome. Makes me feel great!!

All my love forever and ever—

BRENDA

1980

•

From Los Angeles, Henry was doing everything he could to help me set film deals based on his book. He tried to pave the way with telegrams.

•

T#
260305Y PARIS F
003 2358
260406JD PARIR F
= = = =

    MR MICHAEL HOFFMAN   005
    77, BLD SAINT MICHEL
                        75005   PARIS
= = = =

ZCZC SJD542 PSW823 4-05953 4S003
FRXX CO UWNX 076
TDMT PACIFIC PALISADES CA 76/73 03 0555P EST PAGE 01/54

GEORGES HOFFMAN AGHOFF
PARIS

PLEASE TELL BRENDA JUST RECEIVED HER EXTRAORDINARY LETTER
FROM PLANE TODAY. STILL WITHOUT PARIS ADDRESS FOR HER. AD-
DRESS OF MADAME LANGMANN IS LE CAPELLAN 1028 PREVERENGES

(VAUD) SWITZERLAND. BELIEVE DURRELL IS IN SOMMIERES. TRY LINA WERTMULLER FOR EUROPE AND JASON ROBARDS FOR AMERICA. TO HELL WITH WARREN BEATTY. HAS SHE

4-059534s003 GEORGES PAGE 02/19

ANY IDEA WHEN RETURNING. NO WORDS GREAT ENOUGH TO EX-PRESS MY LOVE. IS SHE STILL IN PARIS
    HENRY MILLER

CCL
NNNN#
2603056Y PARIS F
26040JD PARIR F

●

But at home, alone, he was letting go.

●

ODE TO BRENDA IN B-MINOR

Is it true that I never loved
anyone as I do you?

Yes and no, *les deux à la fois.*
Unbelievable.
Tonight my heart aches.
It is suffering the first onslaught
of doubt.
Plus frustration, plus envy,
plus jealousy and so on without end.
It is not a "murmur of the heart"
so much as a dolorous
pain in the heart.
An incurable pain.

Yet it must and will be assuaged.
I like to think that at this very moment—
if you are not in someone's arms—
you are writing me that you
love me dearly.

I would like to think all sorts
of pleasant things, romantic nothings,
frogs croaking in the desert,
the muskrat idling away the night,
et cetera, et cetera.

But the days and nights of the "et cetera"
grow frighteningly shorter.
Doubt clubs them down
with a mere gossamer thought.
Despair takes over, leads to *le néant*,
that terrible impasse
in which nothing blooms any longer
and all turns to rust.
Red, red, rust—the rust of the soul
which we conceal so skillfully
if we conceal it at all.

My heart not only hurts but quivers.
As was wont my prick.

The number "1" of Pythagoras is of no avail,
nor miniature pills of dynamite,
nor concentration,
not even NAM MYO HO RENGE KYO!

Nothing is of any avail.
It is just you and I—
a polar grief,
an anecdote.

THE FAITHFUL ONE

Sunday Jan. 7, 1980

Dear Darling Henry,

I am in New York waiting on a plane to take me home. I had a two hour layover and I wanted to quickly write something from your old home state. It's snowing, freezing cold and I love it. I never did tell you how much I love the snow. I do, you know. It's exhilarating!

I had a very, very long interview with Gilles Costay of *Le Matin*. Georges Hoffman acted as interpreter or translator for me. As the interview took over two hours or so, I really do not know how it came off. But I will have an optimistic viewpoint and expect the best or shall I say, hope for the best.

As you know, when someone is being, translated, one never can tell how the outcome will be. So— A photographer also took my picture as I spoke and ran off a roll of film (for television) after the interview.

Directly after that, I met with François Truffaut and presented him with *Smile* in French. He said he had almost all of your books in his library, but not *Smile*. He had read it long ago, but did not remember the story. I was so impressed with him as a human being. He was shy, and charming, spoke wonderful English although he professed he didn't. Was very humble. Kept asking about you, your health, your state of mind etc.

He is a great admirer of yours. He said he also thinks that *The Devil in Paradise* would be a good film. So let's see if he is at all interested in making a movie about clowns, as he has never attempted the subject before. I was relieved to hear him say that. Once a director touches a certain subject they rarely attempt the same subject again.

Anyway, he is going to write me when he reads the book. Also, I showed him a copy of *Joey* and he loved the picture on the back. I told him that we would send him a copy and, of course, he was delighted.

Eugene Braun-Munk, your publisher, took me for coffee and I felt very protected with him as I do with Durrell. He made me feel very comfortable and said if I needed any assistance in Rome with Fellini or Wertmuller, he could and would help. Isn't that terrific? But, of course, one thing at a time.

Yesterday, I met Edith Sorel for coffee and I really like that lady. She is a typical Frenchwoman in style and charm. We covered many subjects in very little time and got along as though I had known her forever. I really do not think that our meeting was an interview. I think it was simply a meeting. She told me about her interviews with Woody Allen and Truffaut and a few other people and you. She loves you very much as a man and the great mind of our time as everyone else I met also agrees. On my next visit to Paris I do hope to spend time with her. She had just arrived back in

Paris as I was leaving. Great timing, huh. I don't care about the timing because I did have an experience, never, never, to forget. I do hope she liked me! One can never tell.

The greatest help of all was that wonderful, beautiful friend of yours, Lawrence Durrell. I spoke with him on the phone frequently, and it was really due to Durrell that everything turned out so well. He is such a divine person, I do hope to visit him when I return.

I loved Paris with all my heart and Paris loves you. I thank you a million times for making this dream come true as you do all my dreams. You are an angel with a magic wand.

It's time to fly to L.A. now, so I'll close and see you soon. There are no words to express my love for you. Gilles Costay asked exactly what Henry Miller means to me and I answered, *"Everything!"*

Forever yours,

BRENDA

•

Henry was slowly fading, and writing became more and more difficult. And even though we spoke on the phone often, and saw each other occasionally, we still wrote.

•

Jan. 22, 1980

My Forever Henry,

You teach me so-o much. You help me understand Life. You are as close to perfection as a rose. Your will, your spirit, your strength is astounding. I am always in awe of you. You as a man. The most special human being in the whole world. I feel like all the nice happenings in my life are attributed to you. You are firmly cemented in my heart, in my mind, in my soul. The rose that never dies, the light that never goes out.

Now, because of you, I can just let things be as they are. That is really a step up the ladder for me, yes?

Because of you, I deal with the moment, with today. I don't worry about tomorrow, I know it'll be here soon enough. Each day is very precious, especially when I see your face, hold your hands, look in your eyes.

Tony and Val love you very much. I watched Tony look at you yesterday and I could see the love he has for you. I know it is difficult for children and their parents, because there is always a difference of opinion on attitude. It's amusing that the very thing parents dislike in their children is usually a characteristic they dislike in themselves and vice-versa. Tony is leaving soon, have you told him you love him lately? It's not so difficult to say . . . I love you, I love you, I love you. It makes me feel wonderful when I say it to the one I love. I wonder if it does the same for others.

Since Paris, I feel different. I can't really explain the reason, except to say that all the years seemed to come together in my mind. Everything became crystal clear. Especially the importance of just being, being oneself to the fullest.

You make me laugh, you make me cry, you make me fight for what I believe and not question the things I cannot change, but accept them for what they are, people, especially.

I hope the doctor has a good report on your health. And I hope you eat a lot of my chicken soup. I know if you eat well, you will be feeling great in a few days. I know!

This letter is too long for your eyes right now. So, I'll close.

Your watercolors are better than ever, but I'm your greatest fan—

> All my love now and forever—
>
> BRENDA

Sunday Midnight

Darling Brenda—

I haven't been able to go to sleep since talking to you earlier this evening. Too elated, too happy, too everything. You not only have magic in your hands but in your voice, your mind, your whole body. You are something to celebrate, like life itself.

I have just taken Valium and two Anacin, which usually put me to sleep (imaginatively) by your side, preferably in your arms, but not as a fornicator—just a beloved. The longer I know you the deeper grows my respect for you and my certitude that all your wishes will be granted. And I mean—before you are eighty or ninety. It has taken me all these years to achieve whatever success one may put upon my life. Yet, in another sense, I can think of myself as a success coming out of the womb. I came out of one womb to enter another of my own creation. I say this because I think there is a genuine parallel between us in this respect.

Now I begin to feel sleepy.

> Good night dear heart.
> Bless your soul!
>
> HENRY

5/20/80

Dearest Brenda,
— I'm letting Bill write for me — I can't do it.
[ ] I've missed you very much. I would like you to visit me (or rather for you to visit me).

Dearest Brenda—

I'm letting Bill write this letter for me—can't do it.

I've missed you very much. I would like you to visit me (or rather for you to visit me).

(started again—written by Bill)

Dearest Brenda—

I had a letter from Sandi saying that you wanted to get in touch with me that it was about you. I'm very sorry to read what you had to tell me and wondered just what I can do. I suppose you know or surmise that I am not in good shape—that I am off color. I am going to use Einar now for as long a time as I need or can. Everything is too much. I have been away in a sense, not really, but pretending to be travelling. This will sound like a strange letter to you. And it is a strange letter. I realize it.

As far as I know that Lawrence book is going through. If you want you could write and tell Noel Young to send you a copy of the book. And there is a copy of a book about Gurdjieff by Fritz Peters who died the other day.

Dear Brenda, this isn't any kind of letter, I know that. We will have to wait, I guess, for arrival in a better world. I think that's it.

Tonight I will hold *you* in *my* arms.

And leave you *intact*.

H.M.

●

Farewell, my precious Henry.

B.V.

●

September 29, 1980

And now, a man of 87, madly in love with a young woman who writes me the most extraordinary letters, who loves me to death, who keeps me alive and in love (a perfect love for the first time), who writes me such profound and touching thoughts that I am joyous and confused as only a teenager could be. But more than that—grateful, thankful, lucky. Do I really deserve all the beautiful praises you heap on me? You cause me to wonder exactly who I am, do I really know who and what I am? You leave me swimming in mystery. For that I love you all the more. I get down on my knees, I pray for you, I bless you with what little sainthood is in me. May you fare well, dearest Brenda, and never regret this romance in the midst of your young life. We have been both blessed. We are not of this world. We are of the stars and the universe beyond.

Long live Brenda Venus!

God give her joy and fulfillment and love eternal!

HENRY